The Old Nubian Texts from Attiri

Dotawo ▸
Monographs

1

Dotawo ▸ Monographs

Series Editors   Giovanni Ruffini
Vincent W.J. van Gerven Oei

Design   Vincent W.J. van Gerven Oei
Typeset in 10/12 Skolar PE, Lucida Sans Unicode, and Antinoou.

Cover image   Attiri Island, 1964–9 (photo ASSN F/366-3)

Dotawo ▸ is an imprint of punctum books, co-hosted by
DigitalCommons@Fairfield

First published in 2016 by punctum books, Earth, Milky Way.
https://punctumbooks.com/

ISBN-13: 978-0-9982375-7-2
ISBN-10: 0-9982375-7-4
Library of Congress Cataloging Data is available from the Library
of Congress

The Old Nubian Texts from Attiri

Edited by Vincent W.J. van Gerven Oei,
Vincent Pierre-Michel Laisney,
Giovanni Ruffini, Alexandros Tsakos,
Kerstin Weber-Thum, and
Petra Weschenfelder

Contents

Preface

The Old Nubian Texts from Attiri, the first publication in the *Dotawo* ▸ *Monographs* series, presents the first fruits of a new approach to the study of Old Nubian. The Attiri Collaborative, comprising all the scholars who worked on this publication, was born out of the Old Nubian panel at the Nilo-Saharan Linguistics Conference in Cologne in 2013, and took advantage of the generosity of Alexandros Tsakos, who shared with the group the possibility of editing and translating the Old Nubian texts found at Attiri. This collaboration – electronically in 2014 and 2015, in person in Bergen during a workshop from June 1–6, 2015, and finally at the International Medieval Congress in Leeds, July 5, 2016 – demonstrated that the group as a whole, working together, could learn far more from the Attiri texts than any individual scholar working in isolation. This methodology and the results it yielded are a potential model for the editing and translation of any unpublished Old Nubian texts, and present a significant contribution to the study of medieval Nubia.

The Attiri Collaborative would like to thank the Sudan National Museum in Khartoum for granting access to the manuscripts exhibited and stored in its premises so as to procure the photographs with which the work was accomplished and which are published here; David Edwards for supporting Alexandros Tsakos's initial idea for a collective approach to the study of these manuscripts, as well as for material retrieved from A.J. Mills's archive during the process of preparing this publication; the Research Group for Middle Eastern and African Studies at the Institute of Archaeology, History, Cultural Studies and Religion at the University of Bergen for funding the workshop that brought the Attiri collaborators together in June 2015; and finally, Angelika Jakobi, El-Shafie El-Guzuuli, and the Linguistics Department of the University of Khartoum for facilitating Vincent W.J. van Gerven Oei's visit to Khartoum and the Sudan National Museum in February 2016.

List of Tables

List of Figures*

---

*   High-resolution color plates are available through the book website:
    https://punctumbooks.com/titles/the-old-nubian-texts-from-attiri/

Abbreviations

Armbruster: ARMBRUSTER, *Dongolese Nubian: A Lexicon.*
AJM: A.J. Mills's Site Notebooks, part of the ASSN
ASSN: Archaeological Survey of Sudanese Nubia
Copt.: Coptic
D: Dongolawi/Andaandi.
K: Kenzi/Kunuz.
K.: Nicene Canons. BROWNE, *Literary Texts in Old Nubian.*
Khalil: KHALIL, *Wörterbuch der nubischen Sprache.*
L.: Lectionary. BROWNE, *Literary Texts in Old Nubian.*
Lepsius: LEPSIUS, *Nubische Grammatik.*
M.: Miracle of Saint Mina. VAN GERVEN OEI & EL-GUZUULI, *The Miracle of Saint Mina.*
N: Nobiin.
Nauri: GRIFFITH, "The Nubian Texts of the Christian Period," 128–30.
ON: Old Nubian.
P. QI 1: BROWNE & PLUMLEY, *Old Nubian Texts from Qasr Ibrim 1.*
P. QI 2: BROWNE, *Old Nubian Texts from Qasr Ibrim 2.*
P. QI 3: BROWNE, *Old Nubian Texts from Qasr Ibrim 3.*
P. QI 4: RUFFINI, *The Bishop, the Eparch, and the King.*
OND: BROWNE, *Old Nubian Dictionary.*
ONG: BROWNE, *Old Nubian Grammar.*
Reinisch: REINISCH, *Die Nuba-Sprache. Zweiter Theil: Nubisch–Deutsches und Deutsch–Nubisches Wörterbuch.*
SC: Ps.-Chrysostom, In venerabilem crucem sermo. BROWNE, *Literary Texts in Old Nubian.*
SNM: Sudan National Museum
St.: Stauros-Text. BROWNE, *Literary Texts in Old Nubian.*

Editorial Sigla

.	uncertain character
ⲁ̣	ⲁ is uncertain
ⲁ̲	ⲁ is written in red ink
ˋⲁˊ	ⲁ is written above the line
[ⲁ]	ⲁ is reconstructed
<ⲁ>	ⲁ is added by the editor
{ⲁ}	ⲁ is deleted by the editor
[[ⲁ]]	ⲁ is deleted by the scribe
[- - -]	lacuna of unknown number of characters
[1–2]	lacuna of 1 to 2 characters

General Introduction[1]

Attiri is a complex of sites in the Batn el-Hajjar, the rocky area immediately upstream of the Second Cataract, where today the artificial lake created by the Aswan High Dam ends. In the early medieval period, Batn el-Hajjar belonged to the territory of Nobadia, which after the 7th century became the northernmost region of the Makuritan kingdom, the most renowned of the Christian Nubian kingdoms of the Middle Ages. In the end of the medieval era, and, more precisely, from the middle of the 16th century, the region became the southernmost administrative unit of the vast Ottoman Empire.

One of the archeologically more interesting among the sites at Attiri is an island that in the site register of the Sudan Archaeological Map system has the code 16-J-6. Arkell was the first to mention a site on a small island at Attiri back in 1950.[2] He also published an overview photo from a boat trip possibly passing west from the site, in his *History of Sudan*.[3] In both cases he described the mud-brick building on the top of the island as a church, but it is not certain that he made the crossing to the island to verify this observation.

During the Aswan High Dam campaign, Attiri fell under the jurisdiction of the Sudan Antiquities Service and the work was conducted under the direction of A.J. Mills. In his Preliminary Report for 1963–1964, he devoted half a page to listing the principal sites of the locality. Site 16-J-6 was mentioned in Mills's account of the 1963–1964 reconnaissance survey, identified as a Christian village covering the whole island.[4] The field records of Mills's 1964 excavations, however, suggest that the term "village" is hardly applicable to the case of site 16-J-6, the whole known archaeology consisting of about seven buildings.[5]

---

1 This introduction has profited from input and advice by David Edwards.
2 ARKELL, "Varia Sudanica", p. 31.
3 ARKELL, *A History of the Sudan from the Earliest Times to 1821*, pl. 21.
4 MILLS, "The Reconnaissance Survey from Gemai to Dal: A Preliminary Report for 1963–64," pp. 6–7.
5 MILLS, Archaeological Survey of Sudanese Nubia (ASSN) Site Notebook AJM III: pp. 42-43; AJM IX: pp. 56-85.

The records of the excavations are in the largely unpublished archives of the UNESCO-Sudan Antiquities Service survey of the Gemai–Dal region, currently in the partial possession of David Edwards and part of the Archaeological Survey of Sudanese Nubia (ASSN) archive. As for the whole site, W.Y. Adams suggested that "there had been a Late Christian monastic colony on the island," but on the basis of the architectural remains at the site the main period of activity seems to have been the post-Medieval centuries.[6]

The field notes record the finding of 20 fragments of parchment manuscripts (16-J-6/28), 15 of leather (16-J-6/29), and one of paper (16-J-6/34), all unearthed from site 16-J-6 in House IV, magazine 8 from the fill near the entrance.[7] These manuscripts were unearthed on Thursday, December 15, 1966, when the excavation of House IV on the island of Attiri was almost finished. This stratigraphic information seems essential to arrive at an understanding of the date of these documents, which may have been part of a collection during the post-medieval period, or come from the lower (medieval) stratigraphic levels. This issue remains currently unsolved.

The finds were moved to the Sudan National Museum (SNM), and the following concordance was noted on the find cards included in the ASSN archive[8]:

- (16-J-6/28) = SNM 23045
- (16-J-6/29) = SNM 23047
- (16-J-6/34) = SNM 23046

Work at SNM in 2006–8 appears to show that some of these manuscripts have either been misplaced or lost. In more detail:

1. Out of 20 fragments of parchment that comprised find 16-J-6/28 only 10 are registered in Khartoum as SNM 23045.
2. Out of 15 fragments of leather that comprised find 16-J-6/29 only 4 are registered in Khartoum as SNM 23047.
3. The paper fragment with find 16-J-6/34 is registered in Khartoum as parchment under SNM 23046.
4. SNM 23049, another leather manuscript, complete this time, has been registered as coming from Attiri and will be presented in this publication, although its provenance from the complex of sites at Batn el-Hajjar cannot be ascertained.[9]

6   ADAMS, "Islamic Archaeology in Nubia," p. 336.
7   AJM IX: p. 65. One more manuscript, on paper, was found rolled in House V. It is kept in Khartoum as SNM 23048. Thought to be a *hijab*, it has not been part of the present publication.
8   Edwards, p.c.
9   It should be noted that not all manuscripts registered in the SNM as coming from Attiri belong in fact to the collection of finds unearthed by Mills in 1966. SNM 23045 also includes

On February 24, 2016, Vincent W.J. van Gerven Oei autoptically examined the documents catalogued under SNM 23045, 23046, 23047, and 23049 in the depot and exhibition space on the second floor of the Sudan National Museum. It appeared that one document filed under SNM 23045 (here published as P. Attiri 1) was missing or could not be retrieved at that moment. P. Attiri 4 and 11 were on display on the second floor of the museum and readings of the latter could not be verified owing to the suboptimal lighting conditions.

P. Attri 1–2: The Attiri Book of Michael

In an earlier discussion of the Old Nubian texts from Attiri, Alexandros Tsakos proposed that the first three texts presented here form part of a single whole.[10] It now appears, however, that the most damaged of these pages, being also without page number, does not contain any reference to Michael and is instead part of a Lectionary (see discussion below). The other two pages of parchment appear to come from a single codex. Tsakos further proposed, comparing marginal numbers in the Attiri texts against marginal numbers in the Old Nubian *Liber Institutionis Michaelis* from Qasr Ibrim, that both codices are evidence for a medieval Nubian "tradition of compiling codices with works related to Michael."[11] We accept these arguments and present *P. Attiri 1–2* as fragments of a single collection of works on the Archangel Michael, which we propose to call *The Attiri Book of Michael.*

Modern scholars have long been aware of Michael's centrality to Nubian Christianity.[12] The most important literary confirmation of this was the discovery of both a Greek from Serra East[13] and an Old Nubian version from Qasr Ibrim[14] of the central narrative from the so-called *Liber Institutionis Michaelis*, an apocryphal work first identified in two manuscripts from Hamouli in Egypt, one complete in Sahidic and one incomplete in Fayyumic.[15] The two Nubian manuscripts give Nubian and Greek descriptions of Michael's enthronement as governor of heaven (Gr. ἀρχηστράτηγος; Copt.

---

the very well-known Serra East codex with the longest text preserved in the Old Nubian language (SC).

10   TSAKOS, "The *Liber Institutionis Michaelis* in Medieval Nubia," pp. 58–60.
11   Ibid., p. 59.
12   TSAKOS, "The Cult of the Archangel Michael in Nubia."
13   TSAKOS, "The Textual Record from Serra East."
14   BROWNE, "A Revision of the Old Nubian Version of the Institutio Michaelis"; BROWNE, Literary Texts in Old Nubian, pp. 60–62; BROWNE, "An Old Nubian Version of the Liber Institutiones Michaelis"; BROWNE, "Old Nubian Literature," p. 382; BROWNE, "Miscellanea Nubiana (II)," pp. 453–54.
15   MÜLLER, *Die Bücher der Einsetzung der Erzengel Michael und Gabriel*. The central narrative of the *Liber Institutionis Michaelis* appaars in Section 6 of the Coptic vesion as published by Müller.

ⲁⲣⲭⲏⲥⲧⲣⲁⲇⲓⲕⲟⲥ [only in the Fayyumic version]; ON ⲥⲟⲅⲟⲇⲗⲁⲩⲣⲁ) after the fall of Satan.

Moreover, the importance of the cult of Michael is proven by the frequence of the finding of cryptograms, monograms, and full renderings of his name in numerous medieval sites from Nubia.[16] Michael's importance to Nubian piety has even produced funerary stelae from the region between Faras and Meinarti where the Archangel is asked to protect the bones of the deceased.[17] His name has also been found on objects of everyday use.[18] Several other examples of use in monumental iconography[19] underline the primacy of the cult of Michael in Nubia.

Returning to the literary attestations of this cult, it should be stressed that the Old Nubian *Liber* fits squarely within the textual tradition of its Coptic source text.[20] However, the Old Nubian version from Qasr Ibrim seems to be closer to the Greek version from Serra and they should both be considered as creations of the Nubian literary milieus.

Moving to the *Attiri Book of Michael*, we make no systematic attempt to identify the sources of the material in this book. Instead, we prefer to think of it as a set of pervasive and inter-related Michael traditions percolating through medieval Nubia's literary tradition. In part, this is a pragmatic decision: too little of our original codex survives to suppose that we can identify sources with certainty. But as this commentary will show, other factors are at work. The structure of the codex suggests a large number of individual texts, and the structure of the texts suggests that at least one of them may be unique.

One problem complicating the analysis of the *Attiri Book of Michael* is identifying the narrative speaker. The first sentence (1.i.1–3) quotes a speaker addressing Michael directly (signaled by quotation marker -ⲁ̄ on 1.i.3 ⲧⲁⲡⲡⲓⲅⲉⲛⲓⲁ̄ⲁ̄) and describing him as 1.i.2–3 ⲧⲟⲩⲥⲕ̄ⲗ̄ⲗⲱ ⲕⲣ̄ⲣⲁ ⲁ̣ⲓ̈[ⲕⲁ] ⲧⲁⲡⲡⲓⲅⲉⲛⲓⲁ̄- "coming to [the Church of] the Three in order to touch me." A Church of the Three is attested in texts from Qasr Ibrim, which, together with the Church of the Children attested at Banganarti, was apparently in honor of the three youths that God saved from a fiery furnace in the Book of Daniel,

---

16   Perhaps the most characteristic example is the collection of graffiti from the excavations at Soba, see JAKOBIELSKI, "The Inscriptions, Ostraca and Graffiti."

17   VAN DER VLIET, "'What Is Man?,'" p. 198

18   WESCHENFELDER, "Ceramics," 2014, p. 152 and WESCHENFELDER, "Ceramics," 2015, p. 140, discuss different forms in the invocation of Michael on ceramic vessels that were probably applied by their owners by scratching after the firing process.

19   ŁAPTAŚ, "Archangels as Protectors and Guardians in Nubian Painting."

20   BROWNE, "An Old Nubian Version of the *Liber Institutionis Michaelis*," p. 75. See also BROWNE, "A Revision of the Old Nubian Version of the *Institutio Michaelis*," p. 17.

Dan 3:25(92).[21] The introductory sentence of the *Attiri Book of Michael* may then be the words of a priest or lector in a similar Church of the Three, calling on Michael to come to him and using in fact an epithet, 1.i.1 ⲱⲕⲁ̄ ⲁⲁⲩ[ⲁ̄] "Great Ruler," which in Greek is only used for Michael in the context of the story of the three youths in the furnace.[22]

Then, the narrative voice changes. We are no longer in a direct quotation, but are instead in the first-person voice of someone who knows 1.i.3–6 ⲉⲓⲧⲗⲁⲱ ⲅ̄ⲧⲁ ⲁⲩⲧⲁⲕⲁⲣ[ⲁ] ⲙⲟ̄ⲱⲁⲛⲕⲁ "all that has been made silent for man," and who appears to describe humanity as 1.i.10 [ⲁⲛⲛⲁ] ⲧⲟⲩⲫⲓⲅⲟⲩⲗⲗⲱ "children of mine." Are we now hearing the words of Jesus himself being read to the faithful?

In the Qasr Ibrim *Liber Institutionis Michaelis* fragment, a short passage with a third-person narrator introduces the words of Jesus, who thus initiates his disciples to the mysteries that they are eager to learn and ask about. This rhetorical pattern forms a tradition that goes back to the Coptic literary category termed "Diaries of the Apostles" by Joost Hagen.[23] Although it is impossible to ascertain that the present work is such a pseudo-memoir,[24] we may nevertheless expect the possibility that parts of the *Attiri Book of Michael* might work the same way, and contain the words of Jesus as well.

Indeed, this seems true of most of the hair side of page 1. Note the nature of the message in this passage: "all that has been made silent" are secrets that reassure the faithful in response to the 1.i.7–8 ⲙⲁⲛⲧⲁⲕⲗⲱ [ⲉ]ⲛ̄ ⲥⲁⲩⲅⲁⲧⲁ ⲅⲓⲁⲣⲁ̣ⲥ̣ⲛ̄ "when this hateful one [sc. the Devil] was rising." And what follows is Michael's succor – 1.i.10 ⲅⲟⲩ[ⲡⲟⲩⲣⲁ] "shade" and 1.i.15 ⲁⲣⲟⲩⲗⲗⲱ "rain" – to those faithful. Put another way, Jesus delivers a message in which Michael is a central figure of Christianity.[25]

Page 1.ii contains some very insightful remarks about dogma in Christian Nubia. In continuation of Michael's usual presentation as the protector, or 1.ii.5 ⲧⲏⲩⲕⲉⲣ "helper" of the humans awaiting their resurrection while praising God the Father, we read of the Incarnation (1.ii.10 ⲅⲁⲗⲟⲩ ⲉⲕⲕⲁ ⲅⲁⲗⲁⲅⲁ[ⲣⲁ] "became flesh for us"), which is presented rather explicitly: God the Father sent His Son, in pity for the humans, to be born in flesh by the Virgin Mother. The Son's resurrection is the guarantee for the resurrection of the humans, but a prerequisite seems to be a salvation offered by Michael and his God.

---

21 See P. QI 4.78.6 with note *ad loc.* For an overview of known churches in Nubia, see HAGEN, "Districts, Towns, and Other Locations of Medieval Nubia and Egypt."
22 TSAKOS, "The Cult of the Archangel Michael in Nubia."
23 HAGEN, "The Diaries of the Apostles."
24 A term coined by SUCIU, *Apocryphon Berolinense/Argentoratense*, p. 2.
25 It is perhaps worth noting here that for Jehova's Witnesses and Seventh-Day Adventists the Archangel Michael can be identified with Jesus Christ, but we are not aware of any similar belief from Late Antiquity or the Middle Ages.

This sort of salvation is an additional level to the theology of the Orthodox church and reminds us of cosmological battles described in works such as the Manichean and Gnostic treatises.

When we turn to page 2, we are in a radically different section of the *Attiri Book of Michael*. Here, the problem of narrative voice appears even more complex than on page 1. A portion of the page (2.i.1–2, 9–20) is in a neutral third-person voice, but the intervening passage is in direct discourse, in the first person, as the speaker remembers 2.i.2–3 ⲇⲟⲣⲕ̄ⲧⲕⲟⲛ ⲟⲩⲫⲟⲩⲣⲕ̣ⲟ̣ⲩ̣ⲗⲗⲁⲅⲣⲁ̄ · ⲁⲛⲕⲁⲣⲁⲗⲟ "what it was like to be made huffing and puffing in the depth" The speaker is torn, on the one hand inclined to 2.i.4–5 ⲕⲟⲇⲟⲇⲁ ⲧⲟⲕⲁⲣⲣⲉ- "forgive" the sea, and on the other determined to 2.i.8 ⲡⲁⲇⲁⲯⲁ ⲡⲁⲇⲇⲉ̣- "overcome" it.

We are reminded here of Saint Paul, who was three times shipwrecked and spent a day and a night "in the depth of the sea" (2 Cor. 11:25). Is Saint Paul remembering his experiences and deciding whether or not to forgive the depths for what they have wrought on him? This is a plausible interpretation, and the transition from the direct citation in first-person voice (2.i.5 ⲧⲟⲕⲁⲣⲣⲉ̄ⲁ and 8 ⲡⲁⲇⲇⲉ̄ⲁ) to an unnamed "he" in 2.i.9 mirrors the transition after 1.i.3 ⲧⲁⲡⲡⲓⲅⲉⲛⲓⲁ̄ⲁ̄ from direct quotation to an answer of commentary. Perhaps this alternation between direct quotation and explication (in first-person voice on 1.i, in the third-person voice on 2.i) was a guiding narrative strategy in the book, and could possibly indicate that it was supposed to be read by more than one person.

When the first-person voice ends, we read of an unnamed "he" who is 2.i.9 ⲥ̄ⲕⲧⲗ̄ⲗⲱ`ⲉⲛ´ⲇⲉ "neither on earth" 2.i.9–10 ⲧ[ⲟⲩ] ⲥ̣ⲕⲓ̣ⲇ̣ⲕ̣ⲟ̣ⲕⲁ̣ⲧⲧⲗ̄ⲕⲗ̄ ⲟ[1–2]ⲉ̣ⲛ̣ⲇⲉ̣ "nor up to the Trinity," and is someone who acted 2.i.12 ⲧⲓⲗⲗⲁⲅⲗ̄ⲗⲉ "against God." This "he" is the Devil, the devil who appears at the end of the passage (2.i.19 ⲇⲓⲁ̄ⲃⲟⲗⲟⲥⲕⲁ). If the Devil is neither up above nor on earth, then he is in the depths of the sea. There is indeed an apocryphal tradition of that sort. It is preserved in two fragments of Cod. Borg. Copt. 109, fasc. 132 that were identified in 1810 by Zoega as the so-called Acts of Andrew and Paul.[26] There, Paul goes on the boat of a sailor named Apollonios to the deep sea and dives to explore the places were the Lord went. After several miracles caused by the coat of Paul, Andrew goes out on the same boat to bring Paul back from the depths. When he achieves, a series of dialogues begin where Paul first appears speaking with Judas, then narrates what Judas was telling to the Savior, then what Judas was saying to the devil, and in the end what Judas was saying to himself. The important point is that in the depths of the sea,

---

26 Zoega, Catalogus codicum copticorum manu scriptorum qui in Museo Borgeano Velitris adversantur. For an English translation see Alcock, "Two fragments of the Acts of Andrew and Paul (Cod. Borg. Copt. 109, fasc. 132)."

Paul meets Judas as the last prisoner of the devil in Amente (the traditional Egyptian term for the underworld) and even brings back a material token from his visit there, namely a part of the gate of Amente. For the Copts, Amente (ⲁⲙⲛ̄ⲧⲉ) was the commonest name for hell, although the realm of the dead could also be called ⲧⲏ, while the abyss ⲛⲟⲩⲛ.[27] The latter was closest related with the sea, but in general the depths of the hell could be situated either under earth or in the bottom of the sea. In any case, the closest parallels to the imagery of the Attiri passage on the troubles at sea seem to situate us firmly in Paulinian traditions.

Paul is the one who reveals the presence of the devil in the depth of the sea, and in this role he debates the decision to forgive the sea for what it has done, and resolves to overcome it. But how can he alone overcome the sea, where the Devil resides? He can do so only with the help of Michael, who 2.i.14–15 ⲉⲓ. . ⲕⲁ ⲉⲥⲕⲓ̀ ⲧⲁ́ⲕⲁ [[ⲕⲁ]]ⲕⲁⲕⲕⲁ "bears conquered mankind" and 2.i.17–19 ⲧⲁ̀ⲗⲓ̀ ⲗ̀ⲗⲁ ⲧⲱⲉⲕⲧⲉ̣ⲥⲗⲉⲛⲕⲱ · ⲙⲓⲭⲁⲏⲗⲟ ⲁ̅ⲣ̅ⲥ̅ⲥⲁ ⲅⲣ̅ⲣⲁ ⲇⲓⲁⲃⲟⲗⲟⲥⲕⲁ "gave power to God. Michael, excellently casting the Devil." Page 2.i is therefore a striking literary attempt to draw a connection between a well-known New Testament trial of Saint Paul on the one hand and the redemptive power of the Archangel Michael on the other.

Page 2.ii is perhaps the most exciting part of the *Attiri Book of Michael*. In part, this is for theological reasons. Michael's central role in God's creation reaches new heights in these passages. Some of them are obscure. What does it mean to say that Michael 2.ii.1–2 ⲕⲁⲙⲙⲁⲣⲁ ⲡⲛ̄ⲕⲁⲧⲧⲓⲕⲁ "beats pugnacity" or 2.ii.3–4 ⲧⲟⲩ̀ ⲗⲟ́ ⲧⲟⲩⲣⲣⲁ ⲁ̅ⲉⲗ ⲇⲁⲩⲉⲗⲕⲟⲕⲁ "secures the big-hearted inside"? The images are fuzzy and lose something in translation. But some of the passages are quite clear. Michael liberates the enslaved, tramples evil, causes the wise to rule. All of these are deeds that could just as easily be ascribed to Jesus, God Himself, or even Mary, especially in the Catholic tradition.

But perhaps more importantly, these passages seem to suggest a previously unknown literary form, something we may provisionally call a Nubian Alexandrine or dodecasyllable. The first clue comes with the regularity of punctuation and sentence structure. On this page, we have eleven more or less complete sentences and, at the top of the page, the end of a twelfth. All of these sentences share a nearly identical structure: 1) the first word ⲧⲁⲗⲗⲟ, the third person singular personal pronoun with a focus marker, referring (we assume) to Michael; 2) followed – in most cases immediately – by a third-person preterite or present tense verb with a predicative ending; and 3) an object for that verb, invariably with the directive ending -ⲕⲁ.

---

27 Alcock, "From Egyptian to Coptic: Religious Vocabulary."

The result is a striking rhythm, with sentence after sentence rolling through the same sounds: ⲧⲁⲗⲗⲟ <verb>-ⲣ-ⲁ <object>-ⲕⲁ. The Metrical Analysis on pp. 54–55 attempts to provide a systematic approach to the syllabification and prosody of this page.

If indeed page 2.ii is metrically rhythmicized, this fact seems to preclude – or at least dramatically reduce – the possibility of a Greek or Coptic source text for this part of the *Attiri Book of Michael*. It is hard to imagine a Nubian scribe finding such a metrical scheme in a Greek or Coptic source text and contorting his translation to keep the scheme. It is even harder to imagine that a scribe chose this syllable scheme more or less at random and tried to force a translation into it. Finally, can we imagine either option producing a translation with such a tidy ⲧⲁⲗⲗⲟ–ⲣⲁ–ⲕⲁ rhythm, which moreover departs from regular Old Nubian sov structure? On balance, it seems to us most likely that in this portion of the text we have an original Nubian liturgical hymn, dedicated to the Archangel Michael.

In conclusion, the *Attiri Book of Michael* only increases our impression of Michael's importance in medieval Nubia. The two surviving leaves we publish here present at least four different narrative voices, including those of Jesus, Paul, and Michael. Indeed, the rectos and versos of these pages seem to present as many individual and distinct literary texts gathered together to form a whole. If the reconstruction recently presented by Tsakos is correct, then our pages come from a codex perhaps at least 300 pages long.[28] This would suggest that the *Attiri Book of Michael* is a collection of dozens of short, almost bite-size, narratives, prayers, doxologies, poems, and other assorted texts devoted to the Archangel Michael. The scribe responsible for the collection must have had considerable resources at his disposal. If our arguments about the metrical scheme of the final section are accepted, then at least some of this material is original Nubian literature, born not from translation or reception but from indigenous literary talent. This would give the *Attiri Book of Michael* a unique position in the history of Nubian literature, achingly suggestive of what has been lost or what may yet be found.

P. Attiri 3-4: Lectionary (containing Mt 6:25-34, 2 Cor 12)

Both P. Attiri 3 and 4 are fragmentary, and an order between the two pages cannot be established. The texts on both pages allow us to establish the recto and the verso side.

The most complete and satisfying concordance can be established between Mt 6:30–33 and 3.ii.1–11. Considering the mention of the Gospel of Matthew in the incipit on 3.i.7 + ⳝ. ⲉⲩ̄ · ⲙⲁⲟ, it seems

---

28 Tsakos, "The Liber Institutionis Michaelis in Medieval Nubia," 58–59.

logical that 3.ii is the verso side and 3.i.8–14 contains a few verses preceding Mt 6:30. Unfortunately, the recto side is heavily damaged, and our conjecture for starting at Mt 6:25 is based on the fact that this verse starts a new narrative, characterized by the repeated phrase μὴ μεριμνᾶτε/μὴ οὖν μεριμνήσητε. We can thus establish the following matching readings:

P. Attiri 3.i.8–ii.11	Mt 6:25–34	
i.9 ⲅⲟⲗⲁ	25 φάγητε(?)	Table 1. Possible matching readings for P. Attiri 3.i.8–ii.11
ii.1 -ⲉⲓⲟⲛ	30 καὶ	
ii.2 ⲕⲧⲣⲉⲛⲕⲉⲧⲁ̣[ⲗⲗⲉ	30 ἀμφιέννυσιν	
ii.3 ⲡⲉ̣ⲧ[ⲉⲩ	30 (ὀλιγό)πιστοι	
ii.4 ⲙ]ⲁ̣ⲕⲁⲛ ⲁϣϣⲁⲩⲕ[ⲁⲧⲁⲛⲕⲉ	31 μὴ οὖν μεριμνήσητε	
ii.5 -ⲁⲣⲣⲱ	31 (φάγ)ωμεν	
ii.5 ⲙⲛ̄ ⲅ̣ⲉ̣-	31 τί πί(ωμεν)	
ii.6 ⲥⲡ̄ⲡ̣ⲓⲅⲟⲩⲗ	32 ἔθνη	
ii.7 -ⲥⲛ̄	32 γὰρ	
ii.7 ⲟⲩⲛⲛ-	32 ὑμῶν	
ii.8 ⲧ̣ⲟⲩⲥⲕⲁⲛⲧⲉ̣ⲗ[ⲟ	33 πρῶτον	
ii.9 ⲟ]ⲩⲣⲅⲗ ⲉ̄ⲕⲧ̄ⲧⲁⲕⲁⲣ[ⲣⲁ	33 προστεθήσεται ὑμῖν	
ii.10 ⲙⲁⲕⲁⲛ ⲁϣϣⲁⲩ]ⲕⲁⲧⲁⲛⲕⲉ	34 Μὴ οὖν μεριμνήσητε	
ii.11 -ⲟ̄ⲁⲣⲣⲁⲥⲛ̄	34 γὰρ ... (μεριμν)ήσει	

A matching reading with Lk 12:28–32 would also have been possible, were it not that the crucial word πρῶτον/ⲧⲟⲩⲥⲕⲁⲛⲧⲉ̣ⲗ[ⲟ is missing from Lk 12:31. The match between these two passages from Matthew and Luke has been noted from very early in the history of the New Testament. By the fourth century at latest, Eusebius of Caesarea devised a concordance table based on the so-called Ammonian sections that showed the passages that were common between the four canonical Gospels.[29] The Ammonian sections have already been identified by Browne in L. 106.4 and appear in P. Attiri 3.i.7, where we reconstruct ⲙ̄ⲑ̄ as the 49th Ammonian Section. Indeed, in Eusebian tables, section 49 of Matthew equals section 150 of Luke (alias

29 For the Eusebian tables, see Oliver, 'The Epistle of Eusebius to Carpianus." For the Ammonian sections, see Parker, *An Introduction to the New Testament Manuscripts and Their Texts*, 315-16. The Eusebian tables have been used in the 28th edition of the Nestle-Aland, *Novum Testamentum Graece*, Deutsche Bibelgesellschaft. For an online tool, see: http://www.crosswire.org/study/eusebian.jsp?key=Matthew.6.25

Mt 6:25–34 equals Lk 12:22–31.) This perfect match allows us to re-construct without any doubt the reading from Matthew in P. Attiri 3.i–ii as Matthew 6:25-34.

The second page consists of two pieces and is, like P. Attiri 3, heavily damaged on one side. Even though the merging of the two fragments is a major step in the deciphering of the text on the flesh side, it is still too fragmented to provide a definitive clue as to its content. Its character can be quite securely identified as a lectionary based on the reconstruction of lines 4.ii.7 and 4.ii.8, where a refer-ence to a reading from the 4.ii.8 ⲧⲗⲟⲧ̄ⲥ̄ "Apostle" is suggested for a 4.ii.7 ⲛⲧ̄ ⲏⲥ̄ . [1-2]ⲕⲩⲕ̄: . "Sunday of the Lent," as also seen in the Lectionary from Qasr Ibrim (P. QI 1 1.i.4).

The text on the hair side is very fragmented and it does not seem to allow for a possible interpretation of its content. However, the plausible words "deceit" and "brother" can be matched to a read-ing from the Pauline Epistles, as suggested by 4.i.12 ⲁⲡⲥ̄ "Apostle(?)." There is a single reference that seems to offer the correct order and spacing, from the Second Letter to the Corinthians (2 Cor).

Table 2. Possible matching readings for P. Attiri 4.i.13–21

P. Attiri 4.i.13–21	2 Cor 12
19 -ⲁⳝⲱ imperative	16 ἔστω "Be it so"
19 ⲕⲟⲩⲣⲁⲫⲉ "deceit"	16 δόλῳ "guile"
21 ⲉⲓⲣⲁ- "brother"	18 ἀδελφόν "brother"

All attested lectionaries from Nubia preserve the *ordo minor*, which consists of two readings, one from the Epistles from Paul and one from the Gospels, accompanied by a Psalm. However, only one lec-tionary from Nubia preserves a combination of all three, namely a typikon (i.e., a book containing suggestions for readings for each day of a year or a shorter liturgical period, e.g., Great Lent, giving only the beginning and the ending of the suggested passage) from Qasr Ibrim.[30] All the other lectionaries[31] preserve only the readings from Paul and/or from the Gospels.

But another typikon in Greek, identified among three manuscript fragments found in the church of the island of Sur, displays a differ-ent structure. Whereas the joining fragments 9 and 113 preserve only

30 HAGEN & OCHAŁA, "Saints and Scriptures for Phaophi: Preliminary Edition of and Commentary on a Typikon Fragment from Qasr Ibrim."
31 Griffith's lectionary in Berlin: BROWNE, *Griffith's Old Nubian Lectionary*; three lectionaries from Qasr Ibrim now in London: PLUMLEY & BROWNE, *Old Nubian Texts from Qasr Ibrim I*, pp. 22–25 (text no. 5), pp. 28–31 (text no. 7), and BROWNE, "An Old Nubian Lectionary Fragment"; and one lectionary from Sunnarti, now in Heidelberg:

suggestions for readings from Paul and the Gospels[32] on the flesh side of fragment 5,[33] there can be reconstructed a reading from the Epistle of James and a reading from the Acts of the Apostles. This is thus to date the sole evidence for the use of the *ordo maior* in Nubia.

On the hair side of the same fragment, the text preserved proposes a Gospel preceded by either a reading from Paul (2 Cor 13:13) or from the Acts (1:8, 2:38, 4:30, 4:31, 9:31, 13:4, 16:6) and therefore it is not certain whether both sides consist of the *ordo maior* or a combination of the *ordo maior* (flesh side) and the *ordo minor* (hair side). In any case, the Sur-typikon shows that in Nubia there were typika combining the two orders, perhaps according to the type of feast commemorated.[34] An alternative explanation would be that the presentation of the *ordo maior* in the Nubian typika set the readings of the Catholic Epistle and the Acts after those of the Pauline Epistle and the Gospel, which would create a highly original and therefore unlikely liturgical sequence. It should also be noted that the Psalms were not indicated in the Sur typikon, nor in P. Attiri 3. It is probable that special typika were used for the Psalms.[35]

Moving on in more details about P. Attiri 3, it needs to be stressed that this is not a typikon, but a proper lectionary, giving the entire text of the passage to be read in a given day. Until now a reference to a Pauline Epistle and to a Gospel have been confirmed and in this sense it conforms with the other lectionaries in Old Nubian.

If, however, the text of 4 verso is from the Epistle of James rather than from a Pauline Epistle (both equally unsatisfactory, see overleaf), then perhaps the Attiri lectionary contained originally at least some instance of the *ordo maior*. Unfortunately, the text of 3 recto cannot be identified with either a Pauline Epistle (which preceding the Gospel would assign the typikon to the *ordo minor*) or with a passage from the Acts (in which case the typikon would give another instance of the *ordo maior*). The hypothesis is impossible to prove yet and the question of the order used in the Attiri lectionary should remain open.

On the verso page of P. Attiri 4, the two references that seem to resonate with the few words that are fully legible come from the second chapter of the Epistle of James, but the distance between the words that may be reconstructed is larger than one would expect. Based on a selection of the most certain readings, an alternative, but

32   Tsakos, *The Greek Manuscripts on Parchment discovered at site SR022.A in the Fourth Cataract region, North Sudan,* pp. 58–60, 112–13.

33   Ibid., pp. 47–48.

34   Atassanova, "Prinzipen und Kriterien für die Erforschung der koptischen liturgischen Typika des Schenuteklosters," p. 32.

35   Cf. Quecke, "Zwei Blätter aus koptischen Hermeneia-Typika in der Papyrussamlung der Österrichischen Nationalbibliothek (P. Vindob. K 9725 und 9734)."

equally unsatisfying reading, may come from the second chapter of the Pauline Epistle to the Colossians:

Table 3. Possible
matching readings
for P. Attiri 4.ii.9–21

P. Attiri 4.ii.9–21	James 2	Col 2
9 ⲇⲏ̣ⲟ̣ⲩ "to die"		12 νεκρῶν or 13 νεκροὺς "the dead"
10 ⲡⲓⲇⲉ̣ⲣ[]ⲣⲁ̣ⲇ̣- "to beg, pray, be poor"	2 πτωχὸς "poor man"	
13 ⲁⲯⲟ̄ⲓ̈ⲱ̄ "life, Savior"		13 συνεζωοποίησεν "vivify together"
14 ⲧⲟ̣ⲕⲉⲗⲗⲟ̣- "forgive, cease, leave, depart, pass over"		13 χαρισάμενος "gracing"
16 ⲕ̄ⲧ̄ⲡ[]ⲕⲁ "garment, clothing"	3 ἐσθῆτα "clothing"	15 ἀπεκδυσάμενος "despoiling"
20 ⲙⲉⲛⲛⲁⲛⲁⲗⲟ "they don't"	7 οὐκ αὐτοὶ βλασφημοῦσιν "they don't blaspheme"	
21 ⲙⲟ̄ⲱ̣ⲁⲛⲇⲉ "and all the"	10 πάντων "all"	

A final unresolved issue is the meaning of 3.i.13 ⲱⲉⲱ̣ⲱ̣ⲓⲧⲁⲛ̣. There are very few Old Nubian words that begin with a *shai*, which suggests the possibility of a loanword, perhaps related to specific Christian feast particular or with special importance to the region.

A possible candidate would be the Ge'ez cardinal number səssu "six (feminine)" or səssā "sixty" and its ordinal səssāwi(t) "sixtieth."[36] The number six is attested in Old Nubian as ⲅⲟⲇⲟ̄, whereas sixty is not, making this a plausible option. The root would then be either ⲱⲉⲱ̣ⲱⲓⲧ (cf. ⲕⲟⲗⲟⲧ "seven") with an adverbial -ⲁⲛ "sixty times" or ⲱⲉⲱ̣ⲱⲓⲧⲁ (cf. ⲟⲥⲕⲟⲧⲁ "nine") with a genitive -ⲛ "of sixty."

From the incipit in 4.ii.7, we may assume that this Lectionary contained a series of readings associated with the feasts around Lent. A possible candidate would be a feast dedicated to the 60th day before Easter, comparable to the Sexagesima in Catholic liturgy. Without an identified reading of the fragmentary text in 3.ii.14–18, any further conjecture, however, seems impossible.

---

36 Tropper, *Altäthiopisch*, 81, 83, 302.

P. Attiri 5: Unidentified Fragment

The flesh side contains a very fragmented text, where, however, the words might indicate the general nature of the text. If analysed correctly the words 5.i.2 ογρκρο "we/you are hungry," 5.1.4 τōōαρρλ "will give (them)," and 5.i.5 cῆ[πι] ταρο[γ- - -] "blessed nation" point to the text's religious character. The hair side is even more incoherent; not a single word can be determined with any degree of certainty.

P. Attiri 6–7: Fragments

These fragments are too lapidary to make any reasonable conjecture as to their contents or provenance.

P. Attiri 8: The Head

The shape of this dark leather fragment, which appears to contain about 14 lines of writing on one of its sides, seems to have been deliberately shaped in the form of a head by tearing off parts of the manuscript after it had been written. A natural cause for the damage on the edges seems less likely. We are unable to speculate as to the reasons for shaping the document thus. However, other instances of conscious shaping of manuscript fragments in recognizable forms are known from Nubia.[37]

P. Attiri 9: Sale

The strongest clues about the nature of this fragmentary text are the verbal form B.5 παειceλ[o "I wrote" and the mentioning of B.6 τογcκλ *touski* at the end of the text, above the bottom margin. The close proximity of these words strongly suggests that we are dealing here with a legal document of sorts. In all texts in which we have attestations of τογcκ, it either precedes or follows a form of the verb παρ "to write," in which case it indicates the payment of the scribe. When it precedes a form of the verb παρ "to write," but follows a list of names, it indicates the payment of the witnesses. We may compare the extant attestations of τογcκ as follows:

---

37 ŁAJTAR, "Old Nubian Texts from Gebel Adda in the Royal Ontario Museum," p. 198, fig. 6.

Table 4.
Comparison of all
legal documents
mentioning ⲧⲟⲩⲥⲕ

P. Attiri 9.B	Nauri	P.QI 3 32	P. QI 4 69	P. QI 3 36
4 ⲙⲱⲩⲥⲏ	8 ⲙⲁⲧⲁⲣⲓ-ⲅⲟⲩⲗⲗⲟⲛ ... 9 ⲕⲁⲧⲓⲡⲟⲗⲟ (± list of 7 names)	17 ⲙⲁⲧⲁⲣⲓ-ⲅ̅ⲗⲗⲟⲛ ... 22 ⲕⲓⲁ̅ⲕⲱ̅ⲱⲗⲗⲟ (list of 10 names)	14 ⲙⲁⲧⲁⲣⲁ-ⲅⲟⲩⲗⲟ ... 24 ⲓⲟⲁⲛⲛⲟ (long list of names, partially illegible)	i.33 ⲙⲁⲧⲁⲣⲓ-ⲅⲟⲩⲗⲗⲟⲛ ... ii.2 ₽ⲗⲟ (list of 24 names)
			24 ⲧⲟⲩⲥⲕⲏ ⲋ̅·	ii.3 ⲧⲟⲩⲥⲕⲗ̅ ⲡⲁⲧⲓ ⲉ̅ⲗⲟ
5 ⲡⲁⲉⲓⲥⲉⲗ[ⲟ]	9 ⲡⲁⲉⲓⲥⲉ	24 ⲡⲁⲉⲓⲥⲉ	25 ⲡⲁⲓⲉⲓⲥⲉⲗⲟ	ii.6 ⲡⲁⲉⲓⲥⲉ
6 ⲧⲟⲩⲥⲕⲗ̅	11 ⲧⲟⲩⲥⲓ ⲗ̅ⲗ̅ : ⲉⲗⲟ	26 ⲧⲟⲩⲥⲕⲗ̅ ⲅ̅·ⲕⲟ		ii.8 ⲧⲟⲩⲥⲕⲗ̅ ⲡⲁⲧⲓ ⲁ̅ⲗⲟ

All extant documents mentioning ⲧⲟⲩⲥⲕ follow a very similar pattern and are all sales of plots of land. Moreover, all these documents have been written on leather, just like P. Attiri 9. It therefore seems plausible that we are dealing here with a land sale, in which the scribe was paid an unknown amount of ⲧⲟⲩⲥⲕ and one of the witnesses was called ⲙⲱⲩⲥⲏ. The mentioning of A.2 ⲡⲁ[ⲡ]ⲥ̣ⲓⲗ̣ⲟ "bishop" and the (place?) name A.3 -ⲗⲉⲙⲓⲗⲟ may be part of the sequence of dignitaries that usually opens a sale, and it may be possible that the "bishop" is related to the site mentioned in the next line. A.4 ⲧⲁⲡⲗ̅ⲗ̣ⲟ̣ⲛ "his father" might refer to either the buyer or one of the adjacent plot owners, although this remains highly speculative.

P. Attiri 10: Unidentified document

The contents of this document, mentioning measures of food and beverages, as well as a priest, points toward a document of a fiscal character, perhaps an account of some sort.

P. Attiri 11: Letter

The opening words of what otherwise seems to be a list of goods suggest a letter. The sender of the list introduces it with the common letter introduction 1 ⲗⲁⲩⲕⲟⲩⲙⲉⲗⲱ ⲉⲓⲁⲅⲣⲓⲙⲗⲱ "I pay homage (to you). I inform (you)," but continues with a list of items without transition. The contents of the list – as far as we can understand it – are as follows: several domestic animals and different kinds of wine and bread. Different from other lists and accounts that we have in Old

Nubian, this document deviates substantially from the standard form. The following table offers an overview of the structure of the itemized list in 1–5:

Item	Measure	Number	Case
ⲡⲟⲩⲧⲟⲩ	ⲙⲁϣⲉ ⲕⲉⲟⲩⲧ		
ⲕⲓⲁⲇⲓ		H̄	
ⲥⲓⲁⲗⲱ	ⲕⲉⲟⲩⲧ	ⲇ	
ⲥⲩⲕⲙⲓ		ē	ⲗⲱ
ⲥⲩⲣⲕⲓ	ⲙⲟⲣ	ⲇ	
ⲟⲣⲡⲟⲩ		H̄	
ⲕⲟⲡⲁⲧⲟ̄ⲓ		ⲇ	
ⲉⲕⲧⲟⲩ		ⲑ̄	
ⲧⲟⲗⲥⲟⲩ		B̄	
ⲙⲁⲧⲓ̣ⲥ̣ⲕ ⲅⲟⲩⲣⲣⲟⲩ		H̄	
ⲡⲁⲕⲓ			

Table 5. Structure of the itemized list in P. Attiri 11.1–5

Apart from the haphazard way of listing these items, mostly without the otherwise regularly present -ⲗⲱ, the text shows several other idiosyncrasies:

- haplography: 1 ⲇⲁⲩⲕⲟⲩⲙⲉⲗⲱ; 1 ⲉⲓⲁ̣ⲅⲣⲓⲙⲗⲱ; 5 ⲕⲟⲩⲗⲱ and possibly other instances of -ⲗⲗ > -ⲗ
- ⲁⲩ/ⲟⲩ substitution: 1 ⲇⲁⲩⲕⲟⲩⲙⲉⲗⲱ
- ⲇ/ⲧ substitution: 2 ⲕⲓⲁⲇⲓ; 6 ⲁⲑⲓⲧⲓ
- ⲕ/ⲅ substitution: 7 ⲇⲓⲉⲓⲛⲕⲟⲩⲗⲁ;
- ⲟ/ⲟⲩ substitution: 8 ⲕⲣⲉⲛⲟⲧⲟⲣⲁ̣(?)
- phonologically illicit word endings: 2 ⲕⲉⲟⲩⲧ; 4 ⲙⲁⲧⲓ̣ⲥ̣ⲕ

Furthermore, lines 5–8 are extraordinarily difficult to reconstruct. Several words, such as 5, 6 ⲟⲣⲡⲟⲩ "wine"; 7 ⲡⲉ̣ⲧⲉ̣ "dates"; and 7 ⲇⲓⲉⲓⲛⲕⲟⲩⲗⲁ, ⲇⲓⲉⲓⲛⲅⲟⲩⲗ[ⲁ] forms of "to be many" are readily recognizable, but appear grammatically unanchored. There seems to be a verb at the end of the sentence, 8 ⲕⲣⲉⲛⲟⲧⲟⲣⲁ̣, which however has no recognizable form. If we take it to mean something like "coming to deposit," we expect to find a preceding object marked with accusative -ⲕⲁ, for which we find either 6 . ⲕⲁ or 5 ⲇⲁⲇⲕⲁ. Perhaps 6 . ⲕⲁ marks the entire preceding clause 5–6 ⲟⲣⲡⲟⲩ · B̄ · ⲡⲁⲗⲁⲅⲉⲗⲁ · ⲁⲑⲓⲧⲓ · . ⲕⲁ as object, which would possibly explain the aberrant place-

ment of the middot (but cf. 3 cɣκми · ͞є · λω). If we then suppose that
8 κιπιcκο "having eaten" is indeed some type of perfect participial
form, the two constituents 6–7 ορποɣ οcκοɣλλ λιєιnκοɣλλ and 7 πєτє̣
· κοɣλ λιєιnrοɣλ[λ] could be interpreted as adverbative to κιπιcκο.
λλλκλ · κοɣλω, then, is the location where the two amphorae of
wine are supposed to be deposited.

This text appears to be at a remove from the Old Nubian scribal
traditions that we are familiar with. This distance may have been
caused by a lack of education on the part of the scribe or his physical
distance from cultural centers, which could imply dialectal variation. Also, it may be the case that the letter was produced in a period
in which Old Nubian was in general decline. Without a clear idea of
the diachronic development of Old Nubian or its possible dialects,we
are unable to determine whether spatial or temporal distance was
the main cause. Non-standard forms such as 6 πλλλгєλλ; 8 κιπιcκο;
8 κρєnοτορλ̣ seem to indicate a later stage of the language, which
is also confirmed by the petrified and simplified opening formula
1 λλɣκοɣμєλω єιλгριμλω and other particularities indicated above.

A very important implication of the possible identification as
a letter is that this would be the only instance of a letter written
on a leather sheet. Another letter on leather is plausibly identified
among the manuscript fragments discovered in the church of the
island of Sur in the Fourth Cataract region.[38] It is extremely rare to
find Old Nubian documents on leather other than legal texts. Known
exceptions include only P. QI 4.75 (an account). Given the general
idea that leather was a precious and prestigious carrier of text,[39] it is
worth examining whether in this case the scribe simply did not pos-
sess any other possible surface for writing (neither papyrus, paper,
or parchment, which is of no surprise; nor wood, ceramic, or stone,
which is rather peculiar). Can the material nature of the document
indicate something about its meaning, the character of the site, or
the period in which it was written?

38 Tsakos, *The Manuscripts discovered at SR022.A, North Sudan.*
39 Ochała, "Multilingualism in Christian Nubia," pp. 14–15.

Fig. 1. P. Attiri 1.i (SNM 23045). Photo by Alexandros Tsakos.

P. Attiri 1–2
The Attiri Book of Michael

Two folia of a parchment codex with a text written in black and red ink in Old Nubian majuscules by an experienced hand.

P. Attiri 1 (SNM 23045, ±10×15 cm)
i – hair side

   ⲍ̄ⲗ̄

  ⲉ̣ⲓ ⲙⲓⲭⲁⲏ̄ⲗⲓ̈ ⲱⲕⲁ̄ ⲇⲁⲩ[ⲗ̄]

2 ⲧⲟⲩⲥⲕ̄ⲗⲱ ⲕ̄ⲣ̄ⲣⲁ ⲁ̣ⲓ̈[ⲕⲁ]

  ⲧⲁⲡⲡⲓⲅⲉⲛⲓ̈ⲁ̄ⲁ̄ ⲁ̈ⲟ[ⲛ̄ⲣⲓ]

4 ⲅⲟⲩ[.]ⲛⲁ ⲉⲓⲗⲁⲛⲧⲉⲗ̄[ⲟ] ⲉ̣ⲓ

  ⲧⲗ̄ⲇⲱ ⲅ̄ⲧ̄ⲧⲁ ⲁⲩⲧⲁⲕⲁⲣ[ⲁ]

6 ⲙⲱ̄ϣⲁⲛⲕⲁ ⲉⲕ̄ⲕⲁ ⲡⲉⲥ̣[ⲓ]

  ⲛ̇ⲓ̈ⲁ̄ ⲕ̄ⲥ̄ⲥⲉ · ⲛ̇ⲁⲛⲧⲁⲕⲗⲱ

8 [ⲉ]ⲛ̄ ⲥⲁⲩⲅⲁ̄ⲧⲁ ⲅⲓⲁⲣⲁ̄ⲥ̄ⲛ̄ ⲙ̣[ⲓ]

  [ⲭ]ⲁ̣ⲏ̄ⲗⲓ̈ ⲱⲓⲕⲗ̄ ⲇⲁⲩⲉⲗ̄ ⲉ̣ⲛ̄ⲛ̄

10 [ⲁⲛⲛⲁ] ⲧⲟⲩⲯⲓⲅⲟⲩⲗⲗⲱ ⲅⲟⲩ

  [ⲣⲟⲩⲣⲁ] ⲉ̣ⲓⲛⲛ̄ⲅⲟⲩⲛ ⲟ̄ⲟⲩⲣⲓⲁ̄ ⲁⲓ̈ⲁ̄

12 [ⲁⲗ 1–2]ⲧⲟ̣ⲛ̄ⲧⲁⲕⲗ̄ · ⲟⲩⲉⲗⲇⲟ`ⲛ´

  [5–6]ⲟ̣ ⲙⲓⲭⲁⲏ̄ⲗⲓ̈ ⲟⲩϣⲛ̣[ⲟⲛ]

14 [5–6]ⲙⲓⲭⲁ̣ⲏ̄ⲗⲓ̈ ⲥⲛ̄ⲧⲟⲣ ⲧ̣[ ]

  [2–3]ⲕ̣ⲛ̄ ⲁⲣⲟⲩⲗⲗⲱ · ⲡⲁⲡⲕⲁ[- - -]

16 [ⲕⲟⲥ]ⲙⲟⲥⲛ̄ [1–2]ⲅ̣ⲁⲕⲧⲛ̄ ⲅ̣[- - -]

  [2–3]ⲛ̄ ⲧⲁ`ⲩ´ⲕ̣ⲗⲱ · ⲁⲅⲅⲉⲗⲟⲥⲁ

18 [ⲙⲱ̄ϣⲁ]ⲛ̣ⲅⲟⲩⲕⲁ ⲧ̄ⲙ̄ⲓⲅ̣ⲁ

  [ⲣⲁ ⲟ̄]ⲙ̄ⲙ̄ⲗ̄ⲅⲟⲩⲛ ⲡⲁⲡⲕ[ⲁ]

"Oh Michael, Great Ruler, who comes to [the Church of] the Three in order to touch me."

 I came in order to tell you all that has been made silent for man in the completion of times. When this hateful one [sc. the Devil] was rising, Michael the great ruler, who has been […]-ed from me, cast shade upon these children [of mine] because of these things. From one […] Michael sounds […] Michael foundation […] in the rain. […] the father in the time of the […] of the […] of the world, gathering all the angels <while they fight, worshipping> the father of all.

ⲝⲗ̄: 64

1   ⲉⲓ: interjection "oh" (OND 55), introducing a vocative.

ⲙⲓⲭⲁⲏ̄ⲗⲓ̈ ⲱⲕⲁ̄ ⲗⲁⲩ[ⲁ̄]: ⲙⲓⲭⲁⲏ̄ⲗⲓ̈ here and in the rest of the text refers to the archangel Michael, ending, as is characteristic for Old
Nubian names imported from Greek, in a iota. The vocative -ⲁ is
suppressed after names ending in -ⲓ (ONG 3.6.4b). ⲱⲕ[1] (in 9 ⲱⲓⲕ)
here means "ruler" (OND 186[2]) and ⲗⲁⲩ "great" (OND 36). These
epithets are the equivalent of the Greek μέγας ἄρχων, which are
used for Michael only in the context of (references to) the story
of The Three Youths in the Furnace,[3] cf. Michael's epithet in a
fragment from the *Liber Institutionis Michaelis Archangeli* P. QI 1
11.i.1 ⲥⲟⲅⲟⲟ̅ⲁ ⲗⲁⲩⲣⲁⲅⲁ "great eparch." The attributive phrase ⲱⲕ-
ⲁ̄ ⲗⲁⲩ-[ⲁ̄] is marked with the predicative suffix -ⲁ, as is expected
in a vocative context (ONG §3.6.4b[4]). The entire apostrophe ends
in 4 with ⲧⲁⲡⲡⲓⲅⲉⲛⲓⲁ̄ⲁ̄, marked with the final quotation marker
-ⲁ (ONG §4.8).

2   ⲧⲟⲩⲥⲕⲗ̄ⲗⲱ: ⲧⲟⲩⲥⲕ "three" (OND 183), followed by determiner -ⲗ̄[5]
and locative suffix -ⲗⲱ. The reference is here apparently to the
story of three children in Dan 3:25(92), whom, according to the
Coptic and Nubian tradition, were rescued by Michael, as de-
picted in the well-known mural from the Faras cathedral.[6] Considering the locative suffix, perhaps we are dealing here with a
church dedicated to the three children (see the General Introduction, pp 16–17).

ⲕⲣ̄ⲣⲁ: ⲕⲓⲣ "come" (OND 91), with present tense -ⲣ and predicative -ⲁ. The subject is 1 ⲙⲓⲭⲁⲏ̄ⲗⲓ̈.

ⲁⲓ̈[ⲕⲁ]: ⲁⲓ̈ "I," first person singular pronoun with reconstructed accusative case ending -ⲕⲁ, as object of the verb 3 ⲧⲁⲡⲡⲓⲅⲉⲛⲓⲁ̄ⲁ̄.
Apparently ⲁⲓ̈[ⲕⲁ] here is coreferential with the second person
singular 6 ⲉⲕ̄ⲕⲁ.

3   ⲧⲁⲡⲡⲓⲅⲉⲛⲓⲁ̄ⲁ̄: ⲧⲁⲡⲡ-ⲁⲣ "to touch" (OND 165), which should be
analyzed as the root ⲗⲁⲡⲡ followed by transitive suffix -ⲁⲣ, cf.
N *daff* "berühren" (Khalil 110). Because the only two other attestations of this verb show the vetitive ⲧⲁⲡⲡⲁⲧⲧⲁⲙⲏ, with regressive assimilation of the supposedly final -ⲣ of the transitive
suffix, this analysis is not secure. The present form ⲧⲁⲡⲡⲓⲅⲉⲛⲓⲁ̄ⲁ̄

---

1   We have decided to abandon Browne's habit in OND of ending all lemmata in a hyphen.
2   Based on the forms found in this text, the lemma for ⲱⲓⲕⲉⲣⲓ- "ruler" in OND 186 should be
     corrected to ⲱⲓⲕ, pl. ⲱⲓⲕⲉ-ⲣⲓ-. The -ⲣⲓ suffix is attested elsewhere as plural suffix (ONG §3.5.1b).
     Cf. also P. QI 4 93.4 ⲱⲓⲕⲟⲩ and P. QI 4 108.7 ⲱⲓⲕⲁ.
3   TSAKOS, "The Cult of the Archangel Michael in Nubia."
4   New analyses for the variable use of the -a ending in Old Nubian are suggested by
     VAN GERVEN OEI "A Note on the Old Nubian Morpheme -ⲁ" and WEBER-THUM &
     WESCHENFELDER "The Multifunctional -ⲁ."
5   See "A Note on the Grammatical Analysis of the Old Nubian -ⲗ Morpheme," in VAN GERVEN
     OEI, "The Old Nubian Memorial for King George," pp. 256–262.
6   See also the 3D rendering on the Faras 3D website: http://faras3d.pl/galeria/rekonstrukcja/

allows for two solutions. 1) The verbal root should be reanalyzed as ⲧⲁⲡⲡⲁⲅ/ⲧⲁⲡⲡⲓⲅ, which would conform with the previously attested ⲧⲁⲡⲡⲁⲧⲧⲁⲙⲏ. The only other ON bisyllabic verb ending in -ⲅ, ⲫⲟⲩⲣⲟⲩⲅ "to furrow, plough" (OND 185), from *fur* "furrow," has K cognate *burg*, with a final velar absent in *daff*. 2) -ⲓⲅ is a suffix, in which case it can only be an orthographical variant of the habitual -ⲕ,[7] and the ⲕ/ⲅ variation has been attested intervocalically (ONG §2.2.2). This second analysis seems therefore more likely. The suffix -ⲉⲛⲓⲁ̄ is a regular third person singular final (ONG §4.7.7d), and is followed by the quotation marker -ⲁ̄ (ONG §4.8). This verb therefore marks the end of the apostrophe opened by 1 ⲉ̣ⲓ.

ⲁ̈ⲟ[ⲛⲡⲓ]ⲅⲟⲩ[.]ⲛⲁ: previously unattested Greek loanword ⲁ̈ⲟⲛ "eon, time" with reconstructed plural suffix -ⲡⲓ common after Greek loanwords (ONG §3.5.1b), plural suffix -ⲅⲟⲩ and genitive -ⲛⲁ, dependent on 4 ⲉⲓⲗⲁⲛⲧⲉⲗ[ⲟ]. There seems to be a letter between -ⲅⲟⲩ and -ⲛⲁ although grammatically speaking none would be allowed. Although ⲁ̈ⲟⲛ- has not been attested elsewhere (ON usually renders αἰών with ⲉⲗⲗⲉⲛ ⲕⲉⲧⲁⲗⲗⲉⲛ *vel sim.*, see ONG 57), considering the paucity of Old Nubian nouns which could start with ⲁ̈ⲟ- (only certain forms of the first person singular pronoun and abstract compound nouns deriving from ⲁ̄ⲉⲓⲗ "heart"), the semantic context in which ⲉⲓⲗⲁⲛⲧⲉ is regularly used (see below), and the apocalyptic overtones of the text in general, ⲁ̈ⲟ[ⲛⲡⲓ]ⲅⲟⲩ[.]ⲛⲁ seems a plausible reconstruction.

4 ⲉⲓⲗⲁⲛⲧⲉⲗ[ⲟ]: ⲉⲓⲗⲁⲛⲧⲉ "completion" (OND 68), with partially reconstructed locative suffix -ⲗⲟ. Other attestations of this noun are often preceded by a plural noun in the genitive, denoting a temporal unit, e.g., K. 32.6 ⲇⲉ̄ⲗⲅⲟⲩⲛⲁ ⲉⲓⲗⲁⲛⲧⲉⲗⲟ "in the completion of the years" and L. 112.6 ⲧⲁⲩⲟⲩⲕⲅⲟⲩⲛ ⲉⲓⲗⲁⲛⲧⲉⲗⲟ- "in the completion of the times."

ⲉ̣ⲓⲧⲗ̄ⲗⲁⲱ: ⲉⲓⲧ "man" (OND 80), with determiner -ⲗ̄ and suffix -ⲗⲱ "for, upon." There may be room for another letter after the iota at the end of 4, but it would be difficult to conjecture what that might be. The usage of ⲉⲓⲧ "man" as synecdoche for mankind in general has been attested, for example in P. QI 1 9.ii.21 ⲉⲓⲧⲛ̄ ⲧⲟⲧⲛ̄ "of the son of man" (Rev. 14:14).

5 ⲅⲧ̄ⲧⲁ: ⲅⲧ̄ⲧ "to be silent"? (OND 32), with predicative -ⲁ, dependent on 5 ⲁⲩⲧⲁⲕⲁⲣ[ⲁ]. The only other attestation is in K. 25.1 ⲅⲧ̄ⲧⲁ ⲕⲁⲡⲉⲛ "if he eats being silent." Perhaps here used in the sense of "to be unperceivable, hidden."

---

7 Browne insists on the more obscure term "consuetudinal."

ⲁⲩⲧⲁⲕⲁⲣ[ⲁ]: ⲁⲩ "to make" (ⲟⲛⲇ 13), with passive -ⲧⲁⲕ, first preterite -ⲁⲣ, and reconstructed predicative -ⲁ, which is obligatory before the quantifier 6 ⲙⲟ̄ⲱⲁⲛⲕⲁ (ⲟⲛⲅ §3.6.4ⲥ).

6   ⲙⲟ̄ⲱⲁⲛⲕⲁ: ⲙⲟ̄ⲱⲁⲛ "all" (ⲟⲛⲇ 118), with accusative suffix -ⲕⲁ as object of 6 ⲡⲉⲥ[ⲓ]ⲛⲓⲁ̄. 5–6 ⲅ̄ⲧ̄ⲧⲁ ⲁⲩⲧⲁⲕⲁⲣ[ⲁ] ⲙⲟ̄ⲱⲁⲛⲕⲁ may be translated as "all that has been made silent."

ⲉⲕ̄ⲕⲁ: ⲉⲓⲣ "you (sg.)" with accusative suffix -ⲕⲁ, indirect object of 6 ⲡⲉⲥ[ⲓ]ⲛⲓⲁ̄. Coreferential with 2 ⲁⲓ̈[ⲕⲁ]. This implies that the "I" addressing Michael in the first clause is now speaking. It is our conjecture that this person is Jesus himself (see the General Introduction, p. 17).

ⲡⲉⲥ[ⲓ]ⲛⲓⲁ̄: ⲡⲉⲥ "to say" (ⲟⲛⲇ 149) with impersonal final suffix -ⲓⲛⲓⲁ̄, cf. 3 ⲧⲁⲡⲡⲓⲅⲉⲛⲓⲁ̄ⲁ̄.

7   ⲕⲥ̄ⲥⲉ: ⲕⲓⲣ "to come," cf. 2 ⲕⲣ̄ⲣⲁ, with preterite 2 suffix -ⲥ and regressive assimilation of the final *rho* of the root, followed by a first person singular ⲓ + predicative -ⲁ > -ⲉ. This is the main verb of the clause, subordinating the entire final clause 3–7 ⲁⲓ̈ⲟ[ⲛⲡⲓ] ⲅⲟⲩ[.]ⲛⲁ … ⲡⲉⲥ[ⲓ]ⲛⲓⲁ̄.

ⲙⲁⲛⲧⲁⲕⲗⲱ: Grammaticalized complex of distal demonstrative pronoun ⲙⲁⲛ, noun ⲧⲁⲕ from ⲧⲁⲩⲕ "time" (ⲟⲛⲇ 164), and locative -ⲗⲱ. The vowel reduction in ⲧⲁⲕ- and the fact that this constituent is written as a single word are indicative of such a grammaticalization process.[8] Instead of the literal "in that time," we should possibly read simply "when."

8   [ⲉ]ⲛ̄: proximal demonstrative pronoun "this." Considering the noun that it determines, a reading as second person singular genitive pronoun seems unlikely.

ⲥⲁⲩⲅⲁ̄ⲧⲁ: ⲥⲁⲩⲉ̄ "hateful" (ⲟⲛⲇ 156), with nominalizer -ⲁⲧ (ⲟⲛⲅ §3.3.2), "hateful one," followed by the predicative -ⲁ. Reference is made here to the Devil, cf. a fragment from the *Liber Institutionis Michaelis Archangeli* P. QI 1 11.i.16–17 ⲥⲁⲩⲉ̄ⲛ ⲑⲣⲟⲛⲟ[ⲥ …] ⲙⲁⲥⲧⲓⲙⲁ.

ⲅⲓⲁⲣⲁ̄ⲥⲛ̄: ⲅⲓ "to rise" (ⲟⲛⲇ 200), with preterite 1 -ⲁⲣ and predicative -ⲁ, followed by emphatic or focus marker -ⲥⲛ̄, which suggests leftward movement of the temporal subordinate clause 7–8 ⲙⲁⲛⲧⲁⲕⲗⲱ … ⲅⲓⲁⲣⲁ̄ⲥⲛ̄.[9]

9   ⲱⲓⲕⲗ̄ ⲗⲁⲩⲉⲗ̄: "great ruler," cf. 1 ⲱⲕⲁ̄ ⲗⲁⲩ[ⲁ̄] "great ruler." Both words marked with the determiner -ⲗ̄. 8–9 ⲙ[ⲓⲝ]ⲁ̄ⲏ̄ⲗⲓ̈ ⲱⲓⲕⲗ̄ ⲗⲁⲩⲉⲗ̄ is the subject of 9 ⲉⲛ̄ⲛ̄.

ⲉⲛ̄ⲛ̄: either ⲉⲓⲛ "to be" (ⲟⲛⲇ 69), possibly with a third person singular ending, or plural form of the proximal demonstrative pronoun ⲉⲓⲛ, cf. 11 ⲉⲓⲛⲛ̄ⲅⲟⲩⲛ. The manuscript shows more of a superposition of two *nus*, making the ending unclear. The

---

first option, i.e., a form of the copula seems less likely here as we would expect a predicative -ⲁ on the nominal predicate ϣⲓⲕⲗ ⲁⲁⲅⲉⲗ and not a determiner.[10] The second reading seems more plausible, owing to the presence, if reconstructed correctly, of another main verb, 10 ⲅⲟⲩ[ⲣⲟⲩⲣⲁ]. In that case ⲉⲛ̅ⲛ̅ determines 10 ⲧⲟⲩⲯⲓⲅⲟⲩⲗⲁⲱ.

10   [ⲁⲛⲛⲁ]: first person singular possessive pronoun. This seems to be the only logical word before ⲧⲟⲩⲯⲓⲅⲟⲩⲗⲁⲱ and after the demonstrative ⲉⲛ̅ⲛ̅, but any adjective could be possible in theory. The conjecture for a first person is based on the verbal form 7 ⲕⲉ̄ⲥⲉ.

    ⲧⲟⲩⲯⲓⲅⲟⲩⲗⲁⲱ: ⲧⲟⲧ "child," pl. ⲧⲟⲩⲯ (OND 180), with plural suffix -ⲓⲅⲟⲩ, determiner -ⲗ, and suffix -ⲗⲁⲱ "for, upon."

    ⲅⲟⲩ[ⲣⲟⲩⲣⲁ]: ⲅⲟⲩⲣ-ⲟⲩⲣ "overshadow" (OND 204), to be analyzed as ⲅⲟⲩⲣ- "shade" with a reconstructed transitive suffix -ⲟⲩⲣ, and predicative -ⲁ. A reconstruction with the causative, ⲅⲟⲩ[ⲣⲁⲣⲣⲁ], seems equally possible in terms of space, but has not been attested elsewhere as main verb. This shade may be cast by a branch of the cross (St. 12.1–3), "God of the heaven" (P. QI 2 12.ii.8), or a set of wings (P. QI 2 12.ii.20–1). Perhaps in this case, the wings of Michael.

11   ⲉⲓⲛⲛ̅ⲅⲟⲩⲛ ⲟ̄ⲟⲩⲣⲓⲁ̄: plural of the proximal demonstrative pronoun ⲉⲓⲛ followed by the complex postposition genitive + ⲟ̄ⲟⲩⲣⲓⲁ (OND 193), "because of these things."

    ⲁⲓ̈ⲁ[ⲗⲗ]: first person singular pronoun, probably with comitative ⲗⲗ "with," as a reconstruction of ⲁⲓ̈ⲁ[ⲱ] "upon, for me," with the *omega* after the line break would be very uncommon. Also -ⲗ[ⲱ] is less expected with the (unknown) passive verb that follows.

12   -ⲧⲟ̣ⲛ̅ⲧⲁⲕⲗ̄: a participial form ending in a passive suffix -ⲧⲁⲕ and the participial marker/deteminer -ⲗ̄, forming an attributive relative clause dependent on 8–9 ⲙ̅[ⲓⲭ]ⲁⲏ̅ⲗⲓ̈ ϣⲓⲕⲗ̄ ⲁⲁⲅⲉⲗ̄. Another reading may be]ⲅⲣⲡ̅ⲛ̅ⲧⲁⲕⲗ̄, although neither reading seems to conform to any previously attested verb form.

    ⲟⲩⲉⲗⲗⲟˋⲛ́: ⲟⲩⲉⲗ "one" (OND 132) with suffix -ⲗⲟˋⲛ́ "from." The nu is written as a tilde above the final omikron, cf. M. 9.14 ⲁ̄ⲟⲩⲕⲕⲟˋⲛ́.

13   ⲟⲩⲱⲛ̣[ⲟⲛ]: ⲟⲩⲱ(ⲟⲩ)ⲛ "to sound (a trumpet)" (OND 142), with a conjectured third person singular preterite 1 ending.

14   ⲥⲓ̅ⲧⲟⲣ: perhaps a variant of ⲥⲟⲩⲙⲡⲟⲩⲧ/ⲥⲙ̅ⲡⲓⲧ "foundation" and ⲥⲟⲩⲙⲡⲟⲩⲧⲣ̅/ⲥⲙ̅ⲡⲓⲧⲁⲣ "to found" (OND 162), cf. P. QI 4 93.re.3 ⲥⲓⲡⲓⲧⲟⲣ and Ruffini's note *ad loc*. Its grammatical relation with the preceding 14 ⲙⲓⲭⲁⲏ̅ⲗⲓ̈ is not clear.

---

10   Van Gerven Oei, "A Note on the Old Nubian Morpheme -ⲁ," pp. 315–16.

15 ⲕⲛ̄ ⲁⲣⲟⲩⲗⲗⲱ: ⲁⲣⲟⲩ "rain" (ⲟⲛⲇ 19), with determiner -ⲗ and locative -ⲗⲱ, cf. 3 ⲧⲟⲩⲥⲕⲗ̄ⲗⲱ, with either a preceding genitive or
third person singular ending -ⲛ̄. According to Browne's lemma
"rain" is also used metaphorically in the sense of "protection,"
and may thus be semantically related to the "overshadowing"
in 10.

ⲡⲁⲡⲕⲁ: ⲡⲁⲡ "father" (ⲟⲛⲇ 144), with accusative -ⲕⲁ. Object of
an unknown verb.

16 [ⲕⲟⲥ]ⲙⲟⲥⲛ̣̄ [1–2]ⲧ̣ⲁⲕⲧⲛ̄ ⲧ̣[- - -] [2–3]ⲛ̣ ⲧⲁ̀ⲩ́ⲕⲗⲱ: Possibly a series
of genitives all dependent on ⲧⲁ̀ⲩ́ⲕⲗⲱ, "in the time," with the
upsilon inserted later by the scribe, cf. 7 ⲙⲁⲛⲧⲁⲕⲗⲱ. The reconstruction of 16 [ⲕⲟⲥ]ⲙⲟⲥⲛ̣̄ appears certain, as it is the only attested Greek loan word in Old Nubian ending in -ⲙⲟⲥ.

17 ⲁⲅⲅⲉⲗⲟⲥⲁ: Greek loanword ⲁⲅⲅⲉⲗⲟⲥ "angel" followed by the predicative suffix -ⲁ, as it is in the scope of the universal quantifier
18 [ⲙⳝ̄ⲱⲁ]ⲛ̣ⲅⲟⲩⲕⲁ.

18 [ⲙⳝ̄ⲱⲁ]ⲛ̣ⲅⲟⲩⲕⲁ: "all," with preceding predicative, cf. 5–6
ⲁⲩⲧⲁⲕⲁⲣ[ⲁ] ⲙⳝ̄ⲱⲁⲛⲕⲁ. Marked with plural suffix and accusative
-ⲕⲁ, as object of the verb 18 ⲧⲏ̄ⲙⲓⲅⲁ[ⲣⲁ].

ⲧⲏ̄ⲙⲓⲅⲁ[ⲣⲁ]: ⲧⲏ̄ⲙ "to assemble" (ⲟⲛⲇ 172) with causative suffix
-ⲅⲁⲣ, i.e., "to gather," followed by predicative -ⲁ. The subject is
supposedly still Michael.

19 [ⲟ̄]ⲙ̄ⲗ̄ⲅⲟⲩⲛ: ⲟ̄ⲙ̄ⲗ̄ "everyone" (ⲟⲛⲇ 189), with plural -ⲅⲟⲩ and
genitive -ⲛ, dependent on 19 ⲡⲁⲡⲕ[ⲁ].

ⲡⲁⲡⲕ̣[ⲁ]: "father," cf. 15 ⲡⲁⲡⲕⲁ. Object of 1.ii.1 [ⲗⲓ]ⲧ̣ⲁⲣⲁ.

Fig. 2. P. Attiri 1.ii (SNM 23045). Photo by Alexandros Tsakos.

P. Attiri 1 (ꜱɴᴍ 23045, ±10×15 cm)
ii – flesh side

ⲍⲉ

[ⲁⲛ]ⲅ̣ⲁⲣⲁ ⲇⲟⲩⲕⲕⲉⲣⲁⲛ · ·

2 [ⲟⲩ]ⲛ ⲥⲉⲛⲕⲁ ⲟⲩⲧⲣⲁ̅ ⲉ̄ⲧⲁ

ⲟ̣ⲙⲙⲗ̄ⲅⲟⲩⲕⲁ ⲅ̣ⲁ̣ⲉ̣ⲓ

4 [ⲟ̄]ⲉ̣ⲛⲛⲟ ⲕⲥ̄ⲕⲗ̄ⲗⲱ · ⲙ̲ⲓ̲ⲭ̲ⲁ̲

[ⲏ̄]ⲗ̣ⲓ̈ ⲧⲏⲩⲕⲉⲣ ⲙⲁⲩ ⲟⲩⲁⲁⲁⲗ

6 [ⲗ̄]ⲟ̣ · ⲧⲁⲩⲕⲁ ⲙ̄ⲱ̣ⲱⲁⲛⲛⲟ

ⲧ̣ⲁ̣ⲡⲡⲁⲕⲁ ⲇⲟⲩⲕⲓⲟ̅ⲁ ⲥⲉ̣ⲛ̣

8 ⲕⲟⲗ ⲕⲟⲥⲙⲟⲥ ⲟⲩⲁⲧⲧⲟ̣

ⲕⲁ ⲁ̈ⲟ̣ⲁⲁⲁ ⲧⲁⲛ ⲧⲟⲧⲟⲩ

10 ⲅ̣ⲁⲇⲟⲩ ⲉⲕⲕⲁ ⲅⲁⲇⲁⲅⲁ[ⲣⲁ]

ⲟⲩⲛⲛⲟⲩⲧⲁⲕ̄ⲛ̄ ⲟ̄ⲙ̄[ⲙⲟⲩ]

12 ⲅ̣ⲥ̄ⲥⲟⲩ ⲉⲕⲕⲁ ⲧⲟⲟⲩ[ⲟ̅ⲟⲗ]

ⲁⲯ̣ⲟ̅ⲓ̣ⲕⲟⲩⲛⲛⲟⲗ ⲡⲁ̣[ⲣⲑⲉ]

14 ⲛⲟⲥⲗ̄ ⲉⲓⲛⲗ̄ⲁⲟⲩⲗ ⲙ̲[ⲓⲭⲁⲏⲗ]

ⲅ̣ⲥ̄ⲥⲓⲁⲉ ⲧⲁⲛ ⲧⲗ̄ⲁ̣ⲉ̣ⲕ̣[ⲉⲗ]

16 ⲉⲕⲕⲁ ⲁⲩⲗⲟⲥⲓⲟ̅ⲁⲣⲁ ⲙ̄ⲱ̅

ⲱⲁⲛⲕⲁ ⲅ̣[ⲁⲉⲓ]ⲟ̅ⲉ̣ⲥⲛ̄ⲛⲟ̣ [ⲕ̄ⲥ̄]

18 ⲕⲗ̄ⲗⲱ · ⲟ̣ⲁ̣ⲓ̣ⲁ ⲙ̄ⲱ̅ⲱ[ⲁⲛ]

ⲛⲟⲉⲓⲟⲛ ⲅⲉⲛⲅ̣ⲁⲁ̣[ⲁⲁⲛⲁ]

20 ⲙ̲ⲓ̲ⲭ̲ⲁ̲ⲏ̲ⲗ̄ⲓ̈ ⲁⲱ̣ⲱⲁ[- - -]

---

21 + ⲙⲁⲓⲕⲧⲉ̅[ⲅⲟⲩⲉ]

while they fight, worshiping <the father of all>.

Until he resurrects everyone, fulfilling your request, Michael is the help(er) with you, for all time worshiping his father, the one who has sent, pitying the entire world, his born child (and) son who has become flesh for us; all the saints who have ruled over us; the one who has had life; (and) the virgin who is the mother, until he has resurrected all of us whom the holy Michael and his God have saved. And all the sick and afflicted will get blessed. Michael [...] fear [...].

ⲍ︤ⲉ︥: 65

1   [ⲇⲓ]ⲅⲁⲣⲁ: ⲇⲓⲅⲁⲣ "to fight" (ⲟⲛⲇ 46), with predicative -ⲁ, in a multiverb construction with 1 ⲇⲟⲩⲕⲕⲉⲣⲁⲛ.

ⲇⲟⲩⲕⲕⲉⲣⲁⲛ: ⲇⲟⲩⲕ "to worship" (ⲟⲛⲇ 52), with habitual -ⲕ,
present tense suffix -ⲉⲣ and third person plural -ⲁⲛ, the implied
subject being 1.i.17 ⲁⲅⲅⲉⲗⲟⲥⲁ [ⲙ︤ⲟ︦ⲩ︦ⲱ︥ⲁ]ⲛⲅⲟⲩⲕⲁ. The absence of a
predicative suffix indicates that this is a subordinate clause, dependent on and contemporaneous with 1.i.18 ⲧ︤ⲏ︥ⲙⲓⲅⲁ[ⲣⲁ].[1] The
sentence ends uniquely with two middots, suggesting perhaps
a change of speaker.

2   [ⲟⲩ]ⲛ: second person plural genitive pronoun, reconstructed
based on 5 ⲟⲩⲇⲇⲁⲗ.

ⲥⲉⲛⲕⲁ: possibly related to ⲥⲉⲛ "to ask" and ⲥⲉⲛⲧ "request"
(ⲟⲛⲇ 157), even though the terminal tau of the root seems to be
missing before the accusative case. Maybe the same root as 7
ⲥⲉⲛⲕⲟⲗ? Object of 2 ⲟⲩⲧⲣⲁ̅ ⲉ̄ⲧⲁ.

ⲟⲩⲧⲣⲁ̅: ⲟⲩⲧⲣ "to put" (ⲟⲛⲇ 141) with predicative -ⲁ.

ⲉ̄ⲧⲁ: ⲉⲧ(ⲧ) "to receive" (ⲟⲛⲇ 78) with predicative -ⲁ. We are
possibly dealing with the aspectual marker -ⲉⲧ, with uncertain
meaning.[2] Perhaps the meaning here, with the object 2 ⲥⲉⲛⲕⲁ, is
"fully putting," i.e., "fulfilling."

3   ⲟ̣̅ⲙ̅ⲙ̅ⲗ̅ⲅⲟⲩⲕⲁ: "everyone," cf. 1.i.19 ⲟ̅]ⲙ̅ⲙ̅ⲗ̅ⲅⲟⲩⲛ. Object of 3 ⲅⲁⲉⲓ[ⲟ̅]
ⲉ̣ⲛⲛⲟ.

ⲅⲁⲉⲓ[ⲟ̅]ⲉ̣ⲛⲛⲟ ⲕ̅ⲥ̅ⲕⲗ̅ⲗ̅ⲱ: ⲅⲁⲉⲓⲣ "to save" (ⲟⲛⲇ 195). However, it
seems that the form of this verb root is connected to the noun
ⲅⲁⲓ̈ⲉⲣⲣ(ⲉ) "resurrection." Considering the occurrence of 16
ⲁⲩⲗⲟⲥ- "to save" later on this text, perhaps a better translation
of ⲅⲁⲉⲓⲣ- would be "to resurrect." The verb is marked with pluractional suffix -ⲟ̅, referring to the plural object 3 ⲟ̣̅ⲙ̅ⲙ̅ⲗ̅ⲅⲟⲩⲕⲁ,
second/third person singular present ending -ⲉⲛ and locative
suffix -ⲗⲟ as part of the complex postposition -ⲗⲟ ⲕ̅ⲥ̅ⲕⲗ̅ⲗ̅ⲱ "until." The subject is coreferential with 4 ⲙⲓⲭⲁ[ⲏ̅]ⲗⲓ̈.

5   ⲧⲏⲩⲕⲉⲣ: ⲧⲏⲩⲕ(ⲇ)ⲉⲣ "help" (ⲟⲛⲇ 173), cf. P. QI 2 12.ii.7 ⲧⲏⲩⲕⲉⲣⲣⲁ.

ⲙⲁⲩ: note that until 17–18 ⲅ[ⲁⲉⲓ]ⲟ̅ⲉ̣ⲥⲛ̅ⲛⲟ [ⲕ̅ⲥ̅]ⲕⲗ̅ⲗ̅ⲱ there is no
other candidate for a main verb or predicate, there only being a
series of extraposed clauses under 6 ⲇⲟⲩⲕⲓⲟ̅ⲁ. The only remain-
ing, and grammatically satisfying, interpretation of ⲙⲁⲩ is as affirmative -ⲙⲁ, or as Browne calls it, "indicative copulative" suffix (ⲟⲛⲅ §3.9.16b), with the final *upsilon* caused by subsequent

1   An analysis of finite verbal forms according to their use in main and subordinate clauses
    was recently suggested by WEBER-THUM & WESCHENFELDER, "Reflections on Old
    Nubian Grammar." For an interlinear annoted example from Qasr Ibrim see WEBER &
    WESCHENFELDER, "'Orakelpriester' oder 'patrolmen,'" p. 175.
2   Cf. BECHHAUS-GERST, The (Hi)story of Nobiin, p. 150. See for a more nuanced and comparative
    view JAKOBI & EL-GUZUULI, "Semantic Change and Heterosemy of Dongolawi *ed.*"

oγⲁⲁⲁⲗ[λ]ọ. Note that we do not find the predicative marker -ⲁ on 5 ⲧⲏⲩⲕⲉⲣ, which we would otherwise expect.

oγⲁⲁⲁⲗ[λ]ọ: second person plural oγⲣ with comitative -ⲁⲁⲗ and focus marker -ⲗo.

6 ⲧⲁγⲕⲁ: ⲧⲁγⲕ "time," with predicative -ⲁ in the scope of quantifier ⲙ@@ⲁⲛⲛo.

ⲙ@@ⲁⲛⲛo: with locative suffix -ⲗo and progressive assimilation of the *lambda*.

7 ⲧⲁⲡⲡⲁⲕⲁ: ⲧⲁⲡ(ⲡⲁ) "his father" (ONG §3.7.3), with the accusative case as the object of 7 ⲁoγⲕⲓⲟⲇ̄ⲁ. This form also suggests that *contra* Browne's emendation ⲧⲁⲡⲓⲁ- is the correct form in SC 14.8.

ⲁoγⲕⲓⲟⲇ̄ⲁ: ⲁoγⲕ "to worship" with pluractional suffix -ⲟ̄ and predicative -ⲁ. The subject is still 4 ⲙⲓⲭⲁ[ⲏ̄]ⲗⲓ̈. The pluractional suffix may refer to a repeated action "for all time," or (also) refer to the long list of (extraposed) adjuncts, all seemingly dependent on ⲧⲁⲡⲡⲁⲕⲁ: 7–11 ⲥⲉ̣ⲛⲕoⲗ ... oγⲛⲛoγⲧⲁⲕⲛ̄, 11–12 ⲟ̄ⲙ̄[ⲙoγ] ⲉ̄ⲥ̄ⲥoγ ⲉⲕⲕⲁ ⲧ̄ooγ[ⲟ̄ⲟⲗ], 13 ⲁⲯⲟ̄ⲓⲕoγⲛⲛoⲗ, and 13 ⲡⲁ̣[ⲣⲑⲉ]ⲛoⲥ̄ⲗ ⲉⲓⲛⲗ̄ⲗoγⲗ.

ⲥⲉ̣ⲛⲕoⲗ: a nominal interpretation based on the root ⲥⲉⲛ "to send" seems attractive, ending on the morpheme -ⲕo and the determiner -ⲗ. -ⲕo is attested as functional verbal morpheme in conditional contexts (ONG §4.7.5) and may be related to the innovative perfect tense morpheme *-ko* in Nobiin. Provisionally we could translate with "the one who has sent" or "sender." The genitive-marked constituent 8–11 ⲕoⲥⲙoⲥ ... oγⲛⲛoγⲧⲁⲕⲛ̄ is in its entirety dependent on ⲥⲉ̣ⲛⲕoⲗ.

8 ⲕoⲥⲙoⲥ oγⲁⲧⲧọⲕⲁ: ⲕoⲥⲙoⲥ "world" and oγⲁⲧⲧo "entire" (OND 131), with the accusative case as the object of 9 ⲁⲓ̈oⲁⲁⲁ.

9 ⲁⲓ̈oⲁⲁⲁ: cf. SC 13.15 ⲁⲓoⲁⲁ-ⲛⲓⲁ̄ which Browne translates as "in order to pity," relating it to the noun ⲁⲓ̈oⲣ-ⲧ "mercy" (OND 7), with nominalizer -ⲧ. Based on this form and the one encountered here, we may conjecture the verbal root ⲁⲓ̈oⲁⲁ "to pity."

ⲧⲁⲛ: third person singular pronoun in the genitive case, refers to 7 ⲧⲁⲡⲡⲁⲕⲁ.

ⲧoⲧoγ ⲅⲁⲁoγ: ⲧoⲧ "child," and ⲅⲁⲁ "son" (OND 196), antecedents of the attributive relative clause ending in 11 oγⲛⲛoγⲧⲁⲕⲛ̄.

10 ⲉⲕⲕⲁ: accusative of the first person plural inclusive pronoun, object of 10 ⲅⲁⲁⲁⲅⲁ[ⲣⲁ] The fact that we find a first person plural pronoun here in contrast with 2 [oγ]ⲛ and 5 oγⲁⲁⲁⲗ- maybe suggests that we again have a shift of discursive perspective.

ⲅⲁⲁⲁⲅⲁ[ⲣⲁ]: ⲅⲁⲁ "flesh" (OND 24), with inchoative -ⲁⲅ, preterite 1 -ⲁⲣ, and predicative -ⲁ, cf. SC 9.19 ⲅⲁⲁⲁⲅⲉⲥ-. Considering the presence of an object 10 ⲉⲕⲕⲁ, we would expect the appearance of an applicative suffix, for which there is however no space in the lacuna.

11 ογννογτⲁκⲛ̄: participial form of ογⲛⲛ "to bear," with passive
    -ογτⲁκ and genitive -ⲛ̄, marking the end of the relative clause
    dependent on 7 ⲥⲉⲛ̄ⲕⲟⲗ, cf. L. 112.8 ογννογτⲁⲕⲁ.

    ⲟ̄ⲙ[ⲙⲟγ]: an adjectival form of ⲟ̄ⲓⲙⲙⲗ̄ "all," cf. 1.i.19 [ⲟ̄]ⲙ̄ⲙⲗ̄ⲅⲟγⲛ.
    All other attestations of this word place it after the noun, al-
    though here it clearly precedes 12 ⲣ̄ⲥ̄ⲥⲟγ. The reconstruction
    of the ending -ογ is very tentative, owing to a lack of parallel
    examples. This reconstruction also assumes that the final -ⲗ̄ of
    ⲟ̄ⲙⲙⲗ̄ ought to be analyzed as a determiner in all other attesta-
    tions, and not as part of the root.

12 ⲣ̄ⲥ̄ⲥⲟγ: ⲣ̄ⲥ̄ⲥ "holy" (ond 200), antecedent of a relative clause end-
    ing in 12 ⲧⲟⲟγ[ⲟⲟⲗ].

    ⲉⲕⲕⲁ: cf. 10 ⲉⲕⲕⲁ. Object of 12 ⲧⲟⲟγ[ⲟⲟⲗ].

    ⲧⲟⲟγ[ⲟⲟⲗ]: probably related to ⲧⲟγⲁ "to rule over" (ond 179).
    The reconstruction is based on a similar construction in P. QI 2
    17.i.6–7 ⲧⲁⲣ ⲧⲗ̄ⲗⲟγ ⲟ̄ⲓⲙ[ⲙⲗ̄]ⲕⲁ (or perhaps ⲟ̄ⲓⲙ[ⲙⲓ]ⲕⲁ) ⲧⲟⲟγⲟⲟⲗ.

13 ⲁⲫⲟ̄ⲓⲕⲟγⲛⲛⲟⲗ: ⲁⲫⲟ̄ "life" (ond 23) with ⲕⲟγⲛ "to have" (ond 97),
    preterite 1 -o, and determiner -ⲗ, "that which had life." Perhaps
    an epithet for the Holy Spirit, cf. Copt. ⲡⲉⲧⲁⲛⲅⲟ "the one which
    is (making) alive."

    ⲡⲁ[ⲣⲑⲉ]ⲛⲟⲥⲗ̄: Greek loanword ⲡⲁⲣⲑⲉⲛⲟⲥ "virgin" (ond 146),
    with determiner -ⲗ̄.

14 ⲉⲓⲛⲗ̄ⲁⲟγⲗ: possibly consisting of two words, ⲉⲛ̄ "mother" (ond
    72) with determiner -ⲗ̄ and a participial form of the existential
    verb ⲁⲟγ(ⲗ) "to be, exist" (ond 52) with an assimilated deter-
    miner -ⲗ: *ⲁⲟγⲗ-ⲗ > ⲁⲟγⲗ. Attributive to 13 ⲡⲁ[ⲣⲑⲉ]ⲛⲟⲥⲗ̄.

15 ⲣ̄ⲥ̄ⲥⲓⲁⲉ: ⲣ̄ⲥ̄ⲥ "holy" with coordinating particle -ⲁⲉ "and."

    ⲧⲁⲛ: third person singular pronoun genitive, referring to 14
    ⲙ[ⲓⲭⲁⲏⲗ].

    ⲧⲗ̄ⲁⲉⲕ[ⲉⲗ]: ⲧⲗ̄ⲗ- "God" (ond 171) with coordinating particle
    -ⲁⲉⲕⲉⲗ "and." ⲙ[ⲓⲭⲁⲏⲗ] ⲣ̄ⲥ̄ⲥⲓⲁⲉ ⲧⲁⲛ ⲧⲗ̄ⲁⲉⲕ[ⲉⲗ] is the subject of 16
    ⲁγⲗⲟⲥⲓⲟ̄ⲁⲣⲁ.

16 ⲉⲕⲕⲁ: first person inclusive pronoun accusative, cf. 10, 12 ⲉⲕⲕⲁ.

    ⲁγⲗⲟⲥⲓⲟ̄ⲁⲣⲁ: ⲁγ(ογ)ⲗ "to save," with the aspectual suffix -ⲟⲥ
    that often accompanies ⲁγⲗ, pluractional -ⲓⲟ̄, preterite 1 -ⲁⲣ, and
    predicative -ⲁ. The object is 16 ⲉⲕⲕⲁ. The predicative -ⲁ appears
    here in the scope of the universal quantifier 16 ⲙⲟ̄ⲱ̄ⲁⲛⲕⲁ, cf. 6
    ⲧⲁγⲕⲁ ⲙⲟ̄ⲱ̄ⲁⲛⲛⲟ.

    ⲙⲟ̄ⲱ̄ⲁⲛⲕⲁ: object of 17 ⲣ[ⲁⲉⲓ]ⲟ̄ⲉⲥⲛ̄ⲛⲟ̣.

17 ⲣ[ⲁⲉⲓ]ⲟ̄ⲉⲥⲛ̄ⲛⲟ̣ [ⲕⲥ̄]ⲕⲗ̄ⲗⲱ: reconstruction based on 3–4 ⲣⲁⲉⲓ[ⲟ̄]ⲉ̣ⲛ̣ⲛ̣ⲟ
    ⲕⲥ̄ⲕⲗ̄ⲗⲱ, but with preterite 2 suffix -ⲉⲥ which is absent in the lat-
    ter form. The repetition of this phrase creates a ring composi-
    tion signaling the end of this meandering sentence, followed by
    a middot.

18 ọⲁⲓ̣ⲁ̣: except for the first *omicron* a relatively certain reconstruction, from ⲟⲁ(ⲁ) "to be sick" (OND 122), with predicative -ⲁ before universal quantifier ⲙⲱ̄ⲱ[ⲁⲛ]ⲛⲟⲉⲓⲟⲛ.

ⲙⲱ̄ⲱ[ⲁⲛ]ⲛⲟⲉⲓⲟⲛ: "all," ending in the focus marker -ⲗⲟ and conjunction -ⲉⲓⲟⲛ.

19 ⲅⲉⲛⲅⲁ̣ⲁ̣[ⲁ̣ⲁⲛⲁ]: ⲅⲉⲛ "to be good" (OND 27), with causative -ⲅⲁⲣ with partial progressive assimilation from the root-final *nu* and regressive assimilation from the reconstructed intentional suffix -ⲁ.[3] Considering the plurality of the subject and the fact that this is most probably the main verb of the sentence, a reconstruction of third person plural present with predicative -ⲁⲛⲁ seems suitable.

20 ⲁⲱⲱⲁ[: probably related to the verb ⲁⲱⲱⲁⲩⲉⲓ "to fear" (OND 21). Reconstruction remains uncertain.

21 ⲙⲁⲓⲕⲧⲉ̄[ⲅⲟⲩⲉ]: ⲙⲁⲓⲕⲧ̄- "affliction" (OND 109). The final epsilon with supralinear stroke suggests a plural predicative -ⲉ̄ⲅⲟⲩⲉ ending. The word is preceded by four dots arranged in a diamond shape, perhaps indicating an insertion in the main text. If this is the case, arrangement before 18 ⲙⲱ̄ⲱ[ⲁⲛ]ⲛⲟⲉⲓⲟⲛ would be the most logical, considering the predicative.

---

3 Browne refers to this morpheme as the "future tense" (ONG 3.9.7b). Its morphological distribution however suggests that it is a modal marker. See "Remarks toward a Revised Grammar of Old Nubian," p. 178.

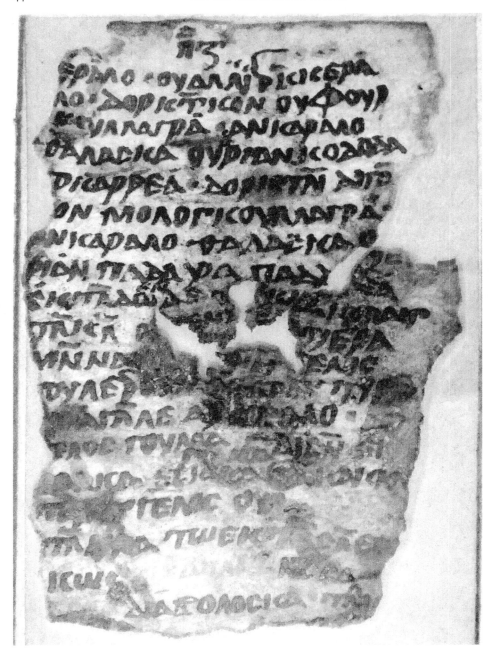

Fig. 3. P. Attiri 2.i (SNM 23045). Photo by Vincent W.J. van Gerven Oei.

P. Attiri 2 (snm 23045, ±10×15 cm)
i – flesh side

    ⲡⲍ̄

    ⲉⲣⲁⲗⲟ · ⲟⲩⲁⲗⲗⲓ̈ⲟ̈ⲕ̄ⲕⲉⲣⲁ

2 ⲗⲟ · ⲇⲟⲣⲕ̄ⲧⲕⲟⲛ ⲟⲩⲫⲟⲩⲣ

    ⲕ̣ⲟⲩⲗⲗⲁⲅⲣ̄ⲁ · ⲁⲛⲕⲁⲣⲁⲗⲟ

4 ⲑⲁⲗⲁⲥⲕⲁ ⲟⲩ`ⲉ´ⲣⲓⲁⲛ ⲕⲟⲇⲟⲇⲁ

    ⲧⲟⲕⲁⲣⲣⲉⲁ̄ · ⲇⲟⲣⲕⲧ̄ⲛ ⲇⲓⲅ̄ⲟ

6 [ⲕ]ⲟⲛ ⲙⲟⲗⲟⲅⲕⲟⲩⲗⲗⲁⲅⲣ̄ⲁ ·

    ⲁ̣ⲛⲕⲁⲣⲁⲗⲟ ⲑⲁⲗⲁⲥⲕⲁ ⲟⲩⲉ̣

8 ⲣⲓⲁⲛ ⲡⲁⲇⲁⲯⲁ ⲡⲁⲇⲇⲉ̣ⲁ̄

    ⲥ̄ⲕⲧⲗ̄ⲇⲱ`ⲉⲛ´ⲇⲉ ⲧ[ⲟⲩ]ⲥ̣ⲕⲓⲇ̣ⲕ̣ⲟ̣ⲕ̣ⲁ̣ⲧ̣

10 ⲧⲗ̄ⲕ̄ⲗ̄ ⲟ[1–2]ⲉ̣ⲛ̣ⲇ̣ⲉ̣ ⲇ̣ⲟⲩⲉ̄ⲣⲁ

    ⲙ̣ⲛ̄ⲛⲁⲗ̣[ⲟ · ⲁ]ⲛ̣ ⲁⲅⲅⲉⲗⲟⲥ

12 ⲅⲟⲩⲗⲉⲟ̄ⲟ̣ⲩ̣ⲛ̣ ⲧⲁ̣ⲣ̣ⲟⲩ ⲧⲓⲗ

    ⲗ̣ⲗ̣ⲁⲅ̄ⲗ̄ⲗⲉ ⲁⲩⲥⲓⲛⲁⲗⲟ · ⲁⲅ

14 ⲅⲉⲗⲟⲥⲅⲟⲩⲗⲗⲁ ⲅ̄ⲁⲓ̈ⲥ̄ⲛ̄ ⲉⲓ

    . . ⲕⲁ ⲉ̣ⲥⲕ̣ⲓ̣`ⲧⲁ´ⲕⲁ [[ⲕ̣ⲁ̣]]ⲕⲁⲕⲕ̣ⲁ̣ ·

16 ⲧⲁ̣ⲣ ⲁ̣ⲅⲅⲉⲗⲟⲥ ⲟⲩⲣ ⲙ̣ⲓ̣ⲭ̣ⲁ̣ⲏ̣ⲗ̣[ⲓ̈]

    ⲧⲗ̄ⲗⲓ`ⲗ´ⲗⲁ ⲧⲱⲉⲕⲧⲥ̄ⲥ̄ⲗⲉⲛ̣

18 ⲕⲱ · ⲙⲓⲭⲁⲏⲗⲟ ⲁ̄ⲅ̄ⲥ̄ⲥⲁ

    ⲅ̄ⲣ̄ⲣⲁ ⲇⲓⲁ̄ⲃⲟⲗⲟⲥⲕⲁ · ⲧⲗ̄`ⲗ´ⲕ̣[ⲁ]

20 [- - -]

[...] he keeps throwing them.

"And having remembered what it was like to be made huffing and puffing in the depth, I [sc. Paul] will on the one hand forgive the sea. But having remembered what it is like tossing and turning in the depth of depths, I will on the other overcome the sea."

He [sc. the devil] is neither upon the earth, nor [...] up to the Trinity. He acted against God concerning my angels.

Who among the angels bears conquered mankind?

Well he, Archangel Michael, who gave power to God. Michael, excellently casting the devil. [...] God [...]

π̅z̅: 87

1　-ⲉⲣⲁⲗⲟ: the final part of a verb form, ending in present tense -ⲉⲣ, predicative -ⲁ, and focus marker -ⲗⲟ.

ⲟⲩⲁⲗⲗⲓⲟ̈ⲕ̅ⲕⲉⲣⲁⲗⲟ: ⲟⲩⲁⲗ "to hurl, throw" (ⲟⲛⲇ 130), followed by pluractional -ⲓⲟ̈, habitual -ⲕ̅ⲕ, present tense, predicative, and focus marker, cf. 1 -ⲉⲣⲁⲗⲟ. The object is plural.

2　ⲁⲟⲣⲕⲧ̅ⲕⲟⲛ: ⲁⲟⲣⲕⲧ̅ "depth" (ⲟⲛⲇ 51), with accusative -ⲕ and conjunction -ⲟⲛ. It is the object of 2 ⲟⲩⲫⲟⲩⲣⲕ̣ⲟ̣ⲩⲗⲗⲁⲅⲣⲁ̅.

The following two sentences have a similar construction, pivoting around 4 ⲟⲩˋⲉ´ⲣⲓⲁⲛ and 7–8 ⲟ̣ⲩⲉ̣ⲣⲓⲁⲛ, here translated as "on the one hand ... on the other" (cf. Greek μέν ... δέ) in both cases followed by a main verb in the first person singular present tense intentional, preceded by a single verb marked with predicative -ⲁ, resp. 4–5 ⲕⲟⲗⲟ̣ⲁⲁ ⲧ̣ⲟⲕⲁⲣⲣⲉ- and 8 ⲡⲁⲗⲁ̣ⲯⲁ ⲡⲁ̣ⲗⲗⲉ̣-. Both parts of the "on the one/on the other" construction are marked at the end with quotation -ⲁ̅, and contain a subordinate clause ending in respectively 3 ⲁⲛⲕⲁⲣⲁⲗⲟ and 7 ⲁⲛⲕⲁⲣⲁⲗⲟ. Note how the construction of starting with a citation followed by a commentary in a different voice is very similar to the rhetorical structure in 1.i.

ⲟⲩⲫⲟⲩⲣⲕ̣ⲟ̣ⲩⲗⲗⲁⲅⲣⲁ̅: a compound verb consisting of ⲟⲩⲫⲟⲩⲣ, a widely attested modern Nubian verb, e.g. N uf "blasen, hauchen, seufzen, schnaufen (vor Hitze)" (Khalil 88), with transitive suffix -ⲟⲩⲣ and ⲕⲟⲩⲗⲗ "to be like" (ⲟⲛⲇ 101[1]), with causative -ⲁⲅⲣ and predicative -ⲁ. ⲁⲟⲣⲕⲧ̅ⲕⲟⲛ ⲟⲩⲫⲟⲩⲣⲕ̣ⲟ̣ⲩⲗⲗⲁⲅⲣⲁ̅ is dependent on ⲁⲛⲕⲁⲣⲁⲗⲟ and could be translated as "to be caused to be like breathing heavily in the depth," here liberally rendered as "what it was like to be made huffing and puffing in the depth."

3　ⲁⲛⲕⲁⲣⲁⲗⲟ: ⲁⲛⲕ "to remember" (ⲟⲛⲇ 12), with preterite 1 -ⲁⲣ and predicative -ⲁ. The subject "I" is implied (see General Introduction, p. 18).

4　ⲑⲁⲗⲁⲥⲕⲁ: Greek loanword ⲑⲁⲗⲁⲥ "sea" (ⲟⲛⲇ 63), with accusative -ⲕⲁ, the object of 4–5 ⲕⲟⲗⲟⲁⲁ ⲧ̣ⲟⲕⲁⲣⲣⲉ-.

ⲟⲩˋⲉ´ⲣⲓⲁⲛ: unattested adverb, related to the root ⲟⲩⲉⲗ "one" (ⲟⲛⲇ 133) and adverb ⲟⲩⲉ̄ⲣⲁⲛ "once" (ⲟⲛⲇ 134). Old Nubian adverbs are often marked with the suffix -ⲁⲛ (ⲟⲛⲅ §3.12). Because of its double occurrence and the semantic contrast between 4–5 ⲕⲟⲗⲟ̣ⲁⲁ ⲧ̣ⲟⲕⲁⲣⲣⲉ- and 8 ⲡⲁⲗⲁ̣ⲯⲁ ⲡⲁ̣ⲗⲗⲉ̣-, we have chosen to translate here with "on the one hand."

ⲕⲟⲗⲟ̣ⲁⲁ: unattested verb ⲕⲟⲗⲟⲁ ending in predicative -ⲁ, possibly related to N kudud "junge, Kind" and kudud-a-ng "klein machen" (Khalil 51) or N kod- "wegradieren" (Khalil 50). Con-

---

1　Browne's ⲟⲛⲇ lemma is ⲕⲟⲩⲗ, but all the extant forms of the verb point to a verbal root ⲕⲟⲩⲗⲗ.

sidering the construction of bare verb root with -ⲁ preceding
the main verb 5 ⲧⲟⲕⲁⲣⲣⲉ-, it is supposed that this verb adds to or
complements the latter's meaning.

5 ⲧⲟⲕⲁⲣⲣⲉⲁ̄: ⲧⲟⲕ- "to forgive" (OND 177), with intentional -ⲁⲗ, and
first person singular present with predicative -ⲡⲉ, followed by
quotation -ⲁ̄.

ⲁⲟⲣⲕⲧⲛ̄ ⲁⲓⲅⲟ̄[ⲕ]ⲟⲛ: ⲁⲟⲣⲕⲧ "depth" with genitive -ⲛ̄, cf. 2
ⲁⲟⲣⲕⲧⲕⲟⲛ, dependent on ⲁⲓⲅⲟ̄[ⲕ]ⲟⲛ, an unattested noun possibly
related to ⲁⲓⲕⲓⲥ "depth" (OND 45) and KD *digire* "fallen, herabfall-
en" (Lepsius 285). With accusative -ⲕ and conjunction -ⲟⲛ, object
of 6 ⲙⲟⲗⲟⲅⲕⲟⲩⲗⲗⲁⲅⲣⲁ̄.

6 ⲙⲟⲗⲟⲅⲕⲟⲩⲗⲗⲁⲅⲣⲁ̄: another compound verb consisting of ⲙⲟⲗⲟⲅ,
an unattested verb, possibly related to cf. N *malgad* "sich krüm-
men, sich drehen, sich wälzen (vor Schmerzen)" (Khalil 70),
and ⲕⲟⲩⲗⲗ "to be like." Cf. 2 ⲟⲩⲫⲟⲩⲣⲕⲟⲩⲗⲗⲁⲅⲣⲁ̄. To highlight the
parallel, the free translation "tossing and turning" was chosen.

7 ⲑⲁⲗⲁⲥⲕⲁ: ⲑⲁⲗⲁⲥ "sea," with accusative -ⲕⲁ, cf. 4 ⲑⲁⲗⲁⲥⲕⲁ. It is the
object of 8 ⲡⲁⲗⲁⲯⲁ ⲡⲁⲗⲗⲉ-.

8 ⲡⲁⲗⲁⲯⲁ: ⲡⲁⲗⲉⲓⲣ "transgress" (OND 143), with predicative -ⲁ.

ⲡⲁⲗⲗⲉⲁ̄: ⲡⲁⲗ "to come out" (OND 143), cf. 5 ⲧⲟⲕⲁⲣⲣⲉⲁ̄. For
the combination ⲡⲁⲗⲁⲯⲁ ⲡⲁⲗⲗⲉⲁ̄, cf. K. 26.13–27.1 ⲧⲉⲗⲟⲩⲧⲟⲩⲕⲁ
ⲡⲁⲗⲉⲓⲫⲁ ⲡⲁⲗⲗⲉⲓⲛⲁ- "he will transgress the laws." Perhaps in
this context, a translation "overtake" or "overcome" makes
more sense. This is the end of the opening citation starting in 1
ⲟⲩⲁⲗⲗⲓⲟ̄ⲕ̄ⲕⲉⲣⲁⲗⲟ, again marked by quotation -ⲁ̄.

9 ⲥ̂ⲕⲧⲗ̄ⲁⲱ`ⲉⲛ´ⲁⲉ: ⲥ̂ⲕⲧ̄ "earth" (OND 77) with determiner -ⲗ̄ and
-ⲁⲱ "upon," followed by conjunction -ⲉⲛⲁⲉ "neither," which
corresponds to 10 -ⲉⲛⲁⲉ "nor."

ⲥ̂ⲕⲧⲗ̄ⲁⲱ`ⲉⲛ´ⲁⲉ ... ⲁⲩⲥⲓⲛⲁⲗⲟ: The subject, explicit in 12 ⲧⲁⲣⲟⲩ,
is supposedly the Devil residing in the depths of the sea, where
he is visited by Paul (see General Introduction, pp. 18–19). The
former is mentioned later explicitly in 19 ⲁⲓⲁ̄ⲃⲟⲗⲟⲥⲕⲁ. As in the
previous clause, which was structured around 4 ⲟⲩ`ⲉ´ⲣⲓⲁⲛ ... 7
ⲟⲩⲉⲣⲓⲁⲛ "on the one hand, on the other," this clause has the repetition 9 -`ⲉⲛ´ⲁⲉ ... 10 -ⲉⲛⲁⲉ "neither, nor."

ⲧ̣[ⲟⲩ]ⲥ̣ⲕ̣ⲓ̣ⲁⲕ̣ⲟⲕ̣ⲁ̣ⲧ̣ⲧⲁ̣ⲕⲗ̄: unattested abstract noun meaning
"Trinity," composed of ⲧⲟⲩⲥⲕⲓⲧ "third" (OND 183), the adjective
formant -ⲕⲟ, and abstract suffix -ⲕⲁⲧⲧ, "third-having-ness" followed by determiner -ⲗ̄ and the suffix -ⲕⲗ̄, attested in -ⲕⲟ̄ⲕⲗ̄ "up
to," which is perhaps the same morpheme as directive -ⲣⲗ̄(ⲗⲉ),
cf. 12 ⲧⲓⲗ̣ⲗ̣ⲁ̣ⲣⲗ̄ⲗⲉ.

10 ⲁⲟⲩⲉ̄ⲣⲁ ⲙ̄ⲛ̄ⲛⲁⲗ[ⲟ: ⲁⲟⲩ(ⲗ) "to be, exist" with present tense -ⲉⲣ and
predicative -ⲁ, in a periphrastic construction with the negative

verb ⲙⲓⲛ (ⲟⲚⲆ 114), and third person singular present plus predicative -ⲛⲁ, followed by focus marker -ⲗⲟ.

11   ⲁ]ⲛ̣: most probably a personal pronoun in the genitive. We have reconstructed here ⲁⲛ "my."

       ⲁⲅⲅⲉⲗⲟⲥⲅⲟⲩⲗⲉⲇⲟ̄ⲅⲛ̣: ⲁⲅⲅⲉⲗⲟⲥ "angel," with plural -ⲅⲟⲩ and suffix -ⲗⲉⲇⲟⲅⲛ "because of, concerning."

12   ⲧⲁ̣ⲣⲟ̣ⲩ: third person personal pronoun.

       ⲧⲓⲗⲗ̣ⲁ̣ⲅ̄ⲗⲉ: ⲧⲗⲗ "God" with dative -ⲗⲁ and directive -ⲅ̄ⲗⲉ, here translated as "against."

13   ⲁⲩⲥⲓⲛⲁⲗⲟ: ⲁⲩ- "to do" (ⲟⲚⲆ 13) with preterite 2 -ⲥ, third person singular -ⲓⲛ, predicative -ⲁ and focus -ⲗⲟ.

       ⲁⲅⲅⲉⲗⲟⲥⲅⲟⲩⲗⲗⲁ: ⲁⲅⲅⲉⲗⲟⲥ "angel," with plural -ⲅⲟⲩ, determiner -ⲗ and dative -ⲗⲁ. Here translated as "among," or "from," dependent on the question word ⲅⲁⲓⲥⲛ̄.

14   ⲅⲁⲓⲥⲛ̄: ⲅⲁⲓ- "who?" (ⲟⲚⲆ 195), with emphatic -ⲥⲛ̄ signaling the leftward movement of the question word (wh-movement.[2] The answer is found in 16 ⲧⲁ̣ⲣ ⲁⲅⲅⲉⲗⲟⲥ ⲟⲩⲣ ⲙⲓⲭⲁⲏⲗ[ⲓ̈].

       ⲉⲓ . . ⲕⲁ: probably a form derived from ⲉⲓⲧ- "man" or ⲉⲧⲕ- "mankind" (ⲟⲚⲆ 80), with accusative -ⲕⲁ, as the object of 15 ⲕ̣ⲁⲕⲕ̣ⲁ̣.

15   ⲉ̣ⲥⲕⲓ̀ⲧⲁ´ⲕⲁ: ⲉⲥⲕ- "to conquer" (ⲟⲚⲆ 61), with passive -ⲓⲧⲁⲕ and predicative -ⲁ, attributive to 14 ⲉⲓ . . ⲕⲁ.

       [[ⲕ̣ⲁ̣]]ⲕⲁⲕⲕ̣ⲁ̣: ⲕⲁⲕ- "to bear" (ⲟⲚⲆ 83), with assimilated present tense -ⲣ and predicative -ⲁ. For the erroneously duplicated and erased ⲕⲁ cf. SC 9.1–3 ⲅⲁⲓⲥⲛ ⲁⲟⲩⲣⲧⲟⲩ ⲅⲁⲇⲕⳝ̄[ⲯⲓⲕⲁ] {ⲕⲁ}ⲕⲁⲕⲕⲁ ⲉⲓⲣⲉⲛ̣ⲁ.

16   ⲧⲁ̣ⲣ: third person singular pronoun, referring to 16 ⲙⲓⲭⲁⲏⲗ[ⲓ̈] ⲁⲅⲅⲉⲗⲟⲥ ⲟⲩⲣ "archangel" (ⲟⲚⲆ 3).

17   ⲧⲗⲗⲓ`ⲗ´ⲗⲁ: ⲧⲗⲗ "God," with determiner -ⲓⲗ and dative -ⲗⲁ. The third lambda is written above the line. Cf. 12 ⲧⲓⲗⲗ̄ⲁ̣ⲅ̄ⲗⲉ.

       ⲧⲱⲉⲕⲧⳡ̣ⲥⲗⲉⲛⲕⲱ: participial form with ⲧⲱⲉⲕ- "power" (ⲟⲚⲆ 177), with benefactive -ⲧⲣ̄ with regressive assimilation of the *rho* before preterite 2 -ⲥ, followed by present tense participial marker/determiner -ⲗ̄ and conjunction -ⲉⲛⲕⲱ "but" (ⲟⲚⲆ 58), here translated with "well." ⲧⲗⲗⲓ`ⲗ´ⲗⲁ ⲧⲱⲉⲕⲧⳡ̣ⲥⲗ̄- is an attributive relative clause depending on 16 ⲧⲁ̣ⲣ ⲁⲅⲅⲉⲗⲟⲥ ⲟⲩⲣ ⲙⲓⲭⲁⲏⲗ[ⲓ̈].

18   ⲙⲓⲭⲁⲏⲗⲟ: with focus marker -ⲟ (which loses the initial lambda after proper names and pronouns)

       ⲁ̄ⲅ̣ⳝ̣ⲥⲁ: ⲁⲅⲓⲥ "to be excellent" (ⲟⲚⲆ 23), with preterite 2 -ⲥ followed by predicative -ⲁ (cf. ⲟⲚⲄ 50 n. 49).

19   ⲅⲣ̄ⲣⲁ: ⲅⲣ̄- "to cast" (ⲟⲚⲆ 32) with present tense -ⲣ and predicative -ⲁ. Cf. 1 ⲟⲩⲁⲗⲗⲓ̈ⲟ̄ⲕ̄ⲕⲉⲣⲁⲗⲟ.

---

2   See Van Gerven Oei, *A Possible Grammar of Old Nubian*.

ⲇⲓⲁⲃⲟⲗⲟⲥⲕⲁ: ⲇⲓⲁⲃⲟⲗⲟⲥ "devil" (ⲟⲛⲇ 44), with accusative, as the object of ⲅⲡ̄ⲣⲁ.

ⲧⲁ`ⲗ´ⲕ̣[ⲁ]: ⲧⲗ̄ⲗ "God," with accusative case, as the object of an illegible verb on the next line.

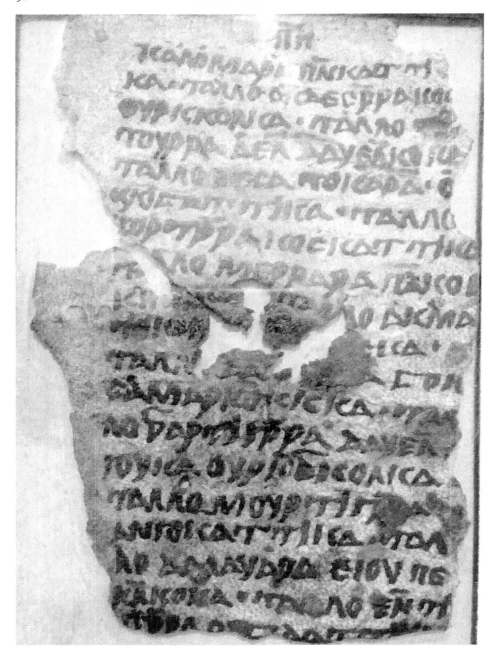

Fig. 4. P. Attiri 2.ii (SNM 23045). Photo by Vincent W.J. van Gerven Oei.

P. Attiri 2 (SNM 23045, ±10×15 cm)
ii – hair side

ⲡ̄ⲏ
ⲕⲁⲙⲙⲁⲣⲁ ⲡ̄ⲛⲕⲁⲧⲧⲓ
2 ⲕⲁ · ⲧⲁⲗⲗⲟ ⲥⲕ̄ⲇⲉⲥⲣ̄ⲣⲁ ⲕⲟⲉ̣
   ⲟⲩⲣⲕⲕⲟⲗⲕⲁ · ⲧⲁⲗⲗⲟ ⲧ̣ⲟ̣ⲩ`ⲗ̣ⲟ́
4 ⲧⲟⲩⲣⲣⲁ ⲇ̄ⲉⲗ̄ ⲇⲁⲅⲉⲗ̄ⲕⲟⲕⲁ ·
   ⲧⲁⲗⲗⲟ ⲇⲉⲥⲁ ⲧⲟⲕⲁⲣⲁ · ⲟ̣̄
6 ⲱⲟⲅ̣ⲁ̣ⲧ̣ⲧⲓⲕⲁ · ⲧⲁⲗⲗⲟ
   ⲕ̣ⲟⲣⲧⲣ̄ⲣⲁ ⲕⲟⲥⲕⲁⲧⲧⲓⲕⲁ[·]
8 ⲧ̣ⲁ̣ⲗⲗⲟ ⲙⲉⲣⲣⲁⲣⲁ ⲡ̄ⲇ̄ⲕⲟⲉ̣
   ⲕ̣ⲓ̣ⲕ̣ . ⲕ̣ⲟ[ⲕⲁ ·] ⲧⲁⲗⲗⲟ ⲁⲕⲏⲁ
10 ⲧ̣ⲓ̣ⲕⲟⲗ [2–3]ⲧ̣ⲟ̣[2–3]ⲥ̣ⲕⲁ ·
   ⲧⲁⲗⲗ[ⲟ] ⲇ̣ⲁ̣ [3–4] ⲁⲅ̣ⲟⲕ̣
12 ⲥⲁⲙⲁⲣⲕⲟⲕⲕⲕⲁ · ⲧⲁⲗ
   ⲗⲟ ⲟ̄ⲁⲣⲧⲓⲅⲣ̄ⲣⲁ ⲇⲁⲅⲉⲗ̄
14 ⲅⲟⲩⲕⲁ ⲟⲩⲣⲕ̄ⲟ̣ⲕⲟⲗⲕⲁ .
   ⲧⲁⲗⲗⲟ ⲙⲟⲩⲣⲧⲓⲅⲣ̄[ⲣ]ⲁ
16 ⲁ̣ⲛⲅⲟⲕⲁⲧⲧⲓⲕⲁ · ⲧⲁⲗ
   ⲗⲟ ⲇⲁⲗⲁⲅⲁⲣⲁ ⲉⲓⲟⲩ ⲡⲉ
18 ⲕ̄ⲁ̄ⲕⲟⲛⲁ · ⲧⲁⲗⲗⲟ ⲉⲛ̄ⲧⲓ
   ⲧ̣ⲣ̄ⲣⲁ̣ ⲟⲩⲧ̣ⲓ̣ⲇⲁ̣ⲧⲧⲓ̣ⲕ̣ⲁ̣

l. 18: read ⲕ̄ⲁ̄ⲕⲟⲕⲁ

[It is he who] [...] beats pugnacity. It is he who overcomes the power-hungry. It is he who secures the big-hearted inside. It is he who liberated the enslaved. It is he who messes up evil. It is he who cuts off [...] . It is he who [...] . It is he who [...] the drunk. It is he who makes those who hunger for great things swear an oath. It is he who causes thoughtfulness to rule. It is he who has made abundant grain glow. It is he who [...] wisdom. [...]

ⲠⲎ: 88

1 ⲕⲁⲙⲙⲁⲣⲁ: unattested form of ⲕⲏⲙ/ⲕⲟⲩⲙⲙ "to beat" (ⲟⲚⲆ 91), with preterite 1 -ⲁⲣ and predicative -ⲁ. Nearly all verbs on this page follow this basic morphological scheme. Considering the syntactical uniformity of the following sequence, it would be safe to assume that the last or penultimate word on the last line of the 2.i is ⲧⲁⲗⲗⲟ.

ⲡⲛⲕⲁⲧⲧⲓⲕⲁ: ⲡⲛ̄ⲕ "to fight" (ⲟⲚⲆ 152) with nominalizer -ⲁⲧⲧ, meaning "pugnacity," and accusative -ⲕⲁ.

2 ⲧⲁⲗⲗⲟ: third person singular personal pronoun ⲧⲁⲣ- with focus marker -ⲗⲟ. Also in 3, 4, 6, 8, 9, 11, 12–13, 15, 16–17, 18. A similar sequence of sentences starting with ⲧⲁⲗⲗⲟ appears in SC 18.5, 9, 10, 12, 25; 19.6, where Browne insistently translates with an English cleft sentence construction "It is he…." The referent in SC is the Cross and in P. Attiri 2.ii is Michael.

ⲥⲕ̄ⲁⲉⲥⲡ̄ⲣⲁ: compound verb of ⲉⲥⲕ "to conquer" (ⲟⲚⲆ 61) and ⲁⲉⲥ "to be free" (ⲟⲚⲆ 43) with present tense -ⲓⲣ and predicative -ⲁ. A possible translation could be "to overcome."

ⲕⲟⲉⲟⲩⲣⲕⲕⲟⲗⲕⲁ: complex participial form consisting of ⲕⲟⲉ̄ "power" (ⲟⲚⲆ 96) and the unattested verb ⲟⲩⲣⲕ "to be hungry," cf. KD *org* "hungern" (Reinisch 134), followed by adjective formant -ⲕⲟ, determiner/present tense -ⲗ, and accusative -ⲕⲁ. A logical translation would be "the power-hungry." Note that the Stauros text has ⲡⲁⲯ(ⲯ) for "to be hungry" (ⲟⲚⲆ 148), related to the N *fañ*. It is unclear whether we are here dealing with synonyms or a dialectal differentiation.

3 ⲧⲟⲩ`ⲗⲟ´: ⲧⲟⲩ "belly" (ⲟⲚⲆ 181) with locative -ⲗⲟ. This form is possibly used adverbially, with the meaning "inside."

4 ⲧⲟⲩⲣⲣⲁ: ⲧⲟⲩⲁ "to be secure" (ⲟⲚⲆ 182[1]) with present tense -ⲣ and predicative -ⲁ.

ⲁⲉⲗ ⲁⲁⲩⲉⲗⲕⲟⲕⲁ: complex adjective consisting of ⲁⲉⲗ "heart" (ⲟⲚⲆ 7) and ⲁⲁⲩⲉⲗ "great" (ⲟⲚⲆ 37), with adjective formant -ⲕⲟ and accusative -ⲕⲁ: "big-hearted."

5 ⲁⲉⲥⲁ ⲧⲟⲕⲁⲣⲁ: ⲁⲉⲥ "to be free," cf. 2 ⲥⲕ̄ⲁⲉⲥⲡ̄ⲣⲁ, followed by ⲧⲟⲕ "to let go," with preterite 1 -ⲁⲣ and predicative -ⲁ. Note the contrast in formation with 2 ⲥⲕ̄ⲁⲉⲥⲡ̄ⲣⲁ, where the two verbs are fully integrated without intervening -ⲁ. Perhaps the reason for this is to be sought in metrical constraints (see Metrical Analysis below). Note also that ⲧⲟⲕⲁⲣⲁ appears to be a preterite form, rather than a present tense.

ⲟ̄ⲱⲟⲥⲁⲧⲧⲓⲕⲁ: ⲟ̄ⲱⲟⲥ "to enslave" (ⲟⲚⲆ 129) with nominalizer -ⲁⲧⲧ and accusative -ⲕⲁ.

---

1 Note that Browne lists ⲧⲟⲩⲁ as an intransitive verb even though it here clearly has an object. So perhaps the lemma in ⲟⲚⲆ should be adjusted.

7 ⲕⲟⲣⲧⲣ̄ⲣⲁ: unknown verb ⲕⲟⲣⲧ, possibly related to N *kurt* "zer-
krümeln, zerbröckeln; trampeln" (Khalil 61), D *kürt* "tangle,
make tangled" (Armbruster 133), and K *kûrt* "umrühren" (Massenbach 192), with transitive -ⲣ̄, present tense -ⲣ and predicative -ⲁ. Here translated with "to mess up," which carries all the
above overtones.

ⲕⲟⲥⲕⲁⲧⲧⲓⲕⲁ: ⲕⲟⲥⲕⲧ̄ⲧ "evil" (ⲟⲛⲇ 100), with accusative -ⲕⲁ.

8 ⲙⲉⲣⲣⲁⲣⲁ: unknown verb, perhaps related to N *merre* "abschnei-
den, abhauen" (Lepsius 362).

ⲡⲁ̄ⲕⲟⲉ̨ⲕⲓⲕ̨ . ⲕ̨ⲟ[ⲕⲁ ·]: unknown simple or complex adjective
with -ⲕⲟ, with reconstructed accusative -ⲕⲁ in the lacuna.

9 ⲁⲕⲙⲁ̨ⲧⲓⲕ̨ⲟ̨ⲗ: perhaps a compound with ⲁⲕ "to sit, remain" (ⲟⲛⲇ
8).

10 -ⲥ̨ⲕⲁ: ending in accusative -ⲕⲁ.

12 ⲥⲁⲙⲁⲣⲕⲟⲕⲕⲕⲁ: ⲥⲁⲙⲁⲣ "intoxication" (ⲟⲛⲇ 156) with verbal root
ⲕⲟ, "to have," participial marker or determiner -ⲗ assimilated
before accusative -ⲕⲁ. The triple *kappa* hardly seems a scribal
error, as the scribe makes generally no mistakes, and has corrected the only one so far, cf. 2.i.15 [[ⲕ̨ⲁ̨]]ⲕⲁⲕⲕ̨ⲁ̨. Perhaps the triple kappa indicates the artifical lengthening of a syllable (see
Metrical Analysis, overleaf).

13 ⲟ̃ⲁⲣⲧⲓⲅⲣ̄ⲣⲁ: unknown verb, possibly related to N *jorti* "Schwur,
Eid," (Khalil 133), sim. KD (Reinisch 61), possibly ending in causative -ⲅⲣ̄, with present tense -ⲣ and predicative -ⲁ.

ⲁ̄ⲁⲩⲉⲗ̄ⲅⲟⲩⲕⲁ: ⲁ̄ⲁⲩⲉⲗ̄ "great," with plural -ⲅⲟⲩ and -ⲕⲁ. The pluractional suffix on ⲟⲩⲣⲕ̄ⲟ̨ⲕⲟⲗⲕⲁ indicate that this is its object.

14 ⲟⲩⲣⲕ̄ⲟ̨ⲕⲟⲗⲕⲁ: ⲟⲩⲣⲕ "to be hungry," with pluractional -ⲓⲟ̃, verbal
root ⲕⲟ, participial marker or determiner -ⲗ, and accusative -ⲕⲁ.
Cf. 2 ⲕⲟⲉ̨ⲟⲩⲣⲕⲕⲟⲗⲕⲁ, which is without pluractional suffix and
with an incorporated object.

15 ⲙⲟⲩⲣⲧⲓⲅⲣ̄[ⲣ]ⲁ: ⲙⲟⲩⲣⲧ "to rule" (ⲟⲛⲇ 121), with causative -ⲓⲅⲣ̄,
present tense -ⲣ, and predicative -ⲁ.

16 ⲁⲛⲅⲟⲕⲁⲧⲧⲓⲕⲁ: possibly composed of ⲁⲛⲅⲟ- from ⲁⲛⲅ "to think, remember" (ⲟⲛⲇ 12), nominalizer -ⲕⲁⲧⲧ, and accusative -ⲕⲁ.

17 ⲁ̄ⲁⲗⲁⲩⲁⲣⲁ: complex verb consisting of ⲁ̄ⲁⲗ "to glow" (ⲟⲛⲇ 34)
and ⲁⲩ "to make," with preterite 1 -ⲁⲣ, and predicative -ⲁ. Cf. SC
18.7 ⲙⲁⳍⲁⲕⲕⲁ ⲁ̄ⲁⲗ ⲁⲩⲁ.

ⲉⲓⲟⲩ: ⲉⲓⲟⲩ "grain" (ⲟⲛⲇ 82).

ⲡⲉⲕⲗ̄ⲕⲟⲛⲁ: read ⲡⲉⲕⲗ̄ⲕⲟⲕⲁ: "to pour in" (ⲟⲛⲇ 148), with determiner -ⲗ̄, verbal root -ⲕⲟ, and accusative -ⲕⲁ. The role of the
determiner before -ⲕⲟ is unclear, but -ⲗ̄ has been attested to in-
tervene, under as yet unknown circumstances (see ⲟⲛⲅ §3.9.13),
between two verbal roots. Perhaps in this case the motivation is
metrical (see Metrical Analysis, overleaf).

18　єⲛ̄ⲧⲓⲧ̄ⲡ̄ⲣⲁ̣: unknown verb, possibly ending in benefactive -ⲓⲧ̄ⲡ̄, present tense -ⲣ, and predicative -ⲁ.

19　ⲟⲩⲅ̣ⲓⲁ̣ⲁⲧⲧⲓⲕⲁ̣: unattested noun "wisdom," possibly a variant of ⲟⲩⲛⲉ "wisdom" (OND 137), ending in nominalizer -ⲁⲁⲧⲧ and accusative case -ⲓⲕⲁ.

Metrical Analysis

The seemingly regular structure of all the clauses on P. Attiri 2.ii, their more or less equal length (twelve units, i.e., a dodecasyllable or Alexandrine), as well as a few curious orthographical features, suggest that their prosodic structure might have been similar, and thus the possibility that these lines may have been chanted or rhythmically recited.

We know very little about Old Nubian phonology and prosody, but robust comparative evidence from other Nile Nubian languages allows us to assume that ON syllables were (C)V(C), with a differentiation between long and short vowels, which however is not marked in the orthography (cf. ONG §2.1.1). However, ON vowel lengths can, as we will see, often be deduced from comparative evidence.

Let us first organize our material under the assumption that the basic unit is a (C)V(C) syllable, where X symbolizes (part of) an unreconstructed syllable:

Table 6. P. Attiri 2.ii organized based on syllable count

	1	2	3	4	5	6	7	8	9	10	11	12	13	14
a	ⲕⲁⲙ	ⲙⲁ	ⲡⲁ	ⲡ̄ⲛ̄	ⲕⲁⲧ	ⲧⲓ	ⲕⲁ							
b	ⲧⲁⲗ	ⲗⲟ	ⲥⲕ̄	ⲁⲉ	ⲥⲡ̄	ⲡⲁ	ⲕⲟ	ⲉ	ⲟⲩⲣⲕ	ⲕⲟⲗ	ⲕⲁ			
c	ⲧⲁⲗ	ⲗⲟ	ⲧⲟⲩ	ⲗⲟ	ⲧⲟⲩⲣ	ⲡⲁ	ⲁ̄	ⲉⲗ̄	ⲁⲁⲩ	ⲉⲗ̄	ⲕⲟ	ⲕⲁ		
d	ⲧⲁⲗ	ⲗⲟ	ⲁⲉ	ⲥⲁ	ⲧⲟ	ⲕⲁ	ⲡⲁ	ⲟ̄	ϣⲟ	ⲅⲁⲧ	ⲧⲓ	ⲕⲁ		
e	ⲧⲁⲗ	ⲗⲟ	ⲕⲟⲣ	ⲧⲡ̄	ⲡⲁ	ⲕⲟⲥ	ⲕⲁⲧ	ⲧⲓ	ⲕⲁ					
f	ⲧⲁⲗ	ⲗⲟ	ⲙⲉⲣ	ⲡⲁ	ⲡⲁ	ⲡⲗ̄	ⲕⲟ	ⲉ	ⲕⲓ	ⲕ̣	X	ⲕ̣ⲟ	[ⲕⲁ]	
g	ⲧⲁⲗ	ⲗⲟ	ⲁⲕ	ⲙⲁ	ⲧⲓ	ⲕⲟ̣ⲗ	X	X	ⲅⲟ̣	X	X	ç	ⲕⲁ	
h	ⲧⲁⲗ	ⲗ[ⲟ]	ⲁⲁ	X	Xⲁ	ⲅⲟⲕ	ⲥⲁ	ⲙⲁⲣ	ⲕⲟⲕⲕ	ⲕⲁ				
i	ⲧⲁⲗ	ⲗⲟ	ⲟ̂ⲁⲣ	ⲧⲓ	ⲅⲡ̄	ⲡⲁ	ⲁⲁⲩ	ⲉⲗ̄	ⲅⲟⲩ	ⲕⲁ	ⲟⲩⲣ	ⲕⲟ̣̄	ⲕⲟⲗ	ⲕⲁ
j	ⲧⲁⲗ	ⲗⲟ	ⲙⲟⲩⲣ	ⲧⲓ	ⲅⲡ̄	[ⲡ]ⲁ	ⲁⲛ	ⲅⲟ	ⲕⲁⲧ	ⲧⲓ	ⲕⲁ			
k	ⲧⲁⲗ	ⲗⲟ	ⲁⲁ	ⲗⲁⲩ	ⲁ	ⲡⲁ	ⲉⲓ	ⲟⲩ	ⲡⲉ	ⲕⲗ̄	ⲕⲟ	ⲛⲁ		
l	ⲧⲁⲗ	ⲗⲟ	ⲉⲛ̄	ⲧⲓ	ⲧⲡ̄	ⲡⲁ	ⲟⲩ	ⲅⲓ	ⲁⲁⲧ	ⲧⲓ	ⲕⲁ			

As we can gather from Table 6, sentences *c*, *d*, *f*, *g*, and *k* have 12 syllables, whereas the others seem to be shorter, with the exception of *i*, which is 14 syllables long. Once we start reconstructing vowel length, however, it seems the pattern becomes more regular. We then need to assume that the basic prosodic unit for this composition is not a syllable but a foot, and that syllables with heavy codas or long vowels count as two feet.

First this means that *b* ⲟⲩⲣⲕ and *h* ⲕⲟⲕⲕ count for two feet, which gives a metrical explanation for the curious triple *kappa* in 12. We also know that the root *e* ⲕⲟⲣⲧ may have a long vowel (cf. KD *kūrt*), as do *g* ⲁⲕ (cf. NKD *āg*) and possibly *h* ⲥⲁⲙⲁⲣ (cf. D *sāmar*). Although *c* already has the correct length, we know that as a noun ⲧⲟⲩ has a long vowel (cf. NKD *tū*), although it may here have been shortened because it is used adverbially, cf. the shortening of 1.i.7 ⲙⲁⲛⲧⲁⲕⲗⲱ.

	1	2	3	4	5	6	7	8	9	10	11	12	13	14
a	[ⲧⲁⲗ	ⲗⲟ]	X	X	X	ⲕⲁⲙ	ⲙⲁ	ⲡⲁ	ⲡⲛ̄	ⲕⲁⲧ	ⲧⲓ	ⲕⲁ		
b	ⲧⲁⲗ	ⲗⲟ	ⲥⲕ̄	ⲇⲉ	ⲥⲡ̄	ⲡⲁ	ⲕⲟ	ⲉ	ⲟⲩⲣⲕ		ⲕⲟⲗ	ⲕⲁ		
c	ⲧⲁⲗ	ⲗⲟ	ⲧⲟⲩ	ⲗⲟ	ⲧⲟⲩⲣ	ⲡⲁ	ⲁ̄	ⲉⲗ̄	ⲇⲁⲩ	ⲉⲗ̄	ⲕⲟ	ⲕⲁ		
d	ⲧⲁⲗ	ⲗⲟ	ⲇⲉ	ⲥⲁ	ⲧⲟ	ⲕⲁ	ⲡⲁ	ⲟ̄	ϣⲟ	ⲥⲁⲧ	ⲧⲓ	ⲕⲁ		
e	ⲧⲁⲗ	ⲗⲟ	ⲕⲟⲣ		ⲧⲣ̄	ⲡⲁ	ⲕⲟⲥ	ⲕⲁⲧ	ⲧⲓ	ⲕⲁ				
f	ⲧⲁⲗ	ⲗⲟ	ⲙⲉⲣ	ⲡⲁ	ⲡⲁ	ⲡⲗ̄ⲁ	ⲕⲟ	ⲉ	ⲕⲓ	ⲕ	X	ⲕⲟ	[ⲕⲁ]	
g	ⲧⲁⲗ	ⲗⲟ	ⲁⲕ		ⲙⲁ	ⲧⲓ	ⲕⲟⲗ	X	ⲅⲟ	X	X ⲥ	ⲕⲁ		
h	ⲧⲁⲗ	ⲗ[ⲟ]	ⲇⲁ	X	X ⲁ	ⲥⲟⲕ	ⲥⲁ		ⲙⲁⲣ	ⲕⲟⲕⲕ		ⲕⲁ		
i	ⲧⲁⲗ	ⲗⲟ	ⲟ̄ⲁⲣ	ⲧⲓ	ⲅⲣ̄	ⲡⲁ	ⲇⲁⲩ	ⲉⲗ̄	ⲅⲟⲩ	ⲕⲁ	ⲟⲩⲣ	ⲕⲟ̄	ⲕⲟⲗ	ⲕⲁ
j	ⲧⲁⲗ	ⲗⲟ	ⲙⲟⲩⲣ	ⲧⲓ	ⲅⲣ̄	[ⲡ]ⲁ	ⲁⲛ	ⲅⲟ	ⲕⲁⲧ	ⲧⲓ	ⲕⲁ			
k	ⲧⲁⲗ	ⲗⲟ	ⲇⲁ	ⲗⲁⲩ	ⲁ	ⲡⲁ	ⲉⲓ	ⲟⲩ	ⲡⲉ	ⲕⲗ̄	ⲕⲟ	ⲛⲁ		
l	ⲧⲁⲗ	ⲗⲟ	ⲉⲛ̄	ⲧⲓ	ⲧⲣ̄	ⲡⲁ	ⲟⲩ		ⲗⲓ	ⲇⲁⲧ	ⲧⲓ	ⲕⲁ		

Table 7. P. Attiri 2.ii organized by feet

Table 7 gives a much more regular pattern, which suggests that vowel length and complex codas were taken into consideration when composing rhythmicized text. It also offers a possible explanation for certain orthographical features of this text, and perhaps accounts for stylistic choices such as the complex verb construction 2 ⲥⲕ̄ⲇⲉⲥⲡ̄ⲣⲁ in contrast with the multiverb construction 5 ⲇⲉⲥⲁ ⲧⲟⲕⲁⲣⲁ. Note also that in *g* feet 9 and 10 can be interchanged, as the lacunae on both sides are 2–3 characters long. Moreover, filling out *a* suggests that there is another word on the previous page, perhaps a verb ending in predicative -ⲁ between reconstructed ⲧⲁⲗⲗⲟ and 1 ⲕⲁⲙⲙⲁⲣⲁ.

What appears is a remarkably even distribution of certain syllables in specific positions throughout all twelve lines. First is the consistent appearance of ⲧⲁⲗⲗⲟ as the first two syllables, but also ⲧⲓ as fourth syllable in *i, j, l*; -ⲣ as fifth in *b, c, e, i, j, l*; -ⲁ as sixth in *b, c, d, e, i, j, k, l*; ⲕ- as eleventh in *b, c, f, j, k*; and ⲕⲁ as twelfth in *a, b, c, d, f, g, h, l.* All of this strongly suggests the presence of a specific rhyming scheme, or at least a composition technique that took the sound quality of the text into account.

These results, however, remain speculative until more is understood about both Old Nubian phonology and Nubian traditions of oral delivery.

Fig. 5. P. Attiri 3.i (SNM 23045). Photo by Vincent W.J. van Gerven Oei.

P. Attiri 3–4
Lectionary

Two folia of a parchment codex with a text written in black and red ink in Old Nubian majuscules.

P. Attiri 3 (SNM 23045, ±5×10 cm)
i – hair side

      OZ̄

    [- - -]ιc̄ χ̄ϲⲗⲁϵ ϵιⲛ̄ . . [- - -]

2   [- - -] . κ̄ ⲛⲁκⲁ ⲧ . [- - -]

    [- - -] . ⲛ̄ⲅⲟⲩⲗⲁ ⲇⲟⲩⲗⲗ[- - -]

4   [- - -] ⲟⲩκⲁ ⲧ̄ⲟ̄ⲟ̄ⲁ . [- - -]

    [- - -]ⲇⲟⲗⲗιⲣⲟ . κ̄[- - -]

6   [- - -] . . ⲧⲉⲇⲇⲁⲗ ⲁⲧ[- - -]

    [- - -] + . ϵⲩ̄ · ⲙⲁθ · ⲙ[θ - -]

8   [- - -] . . ϵⲛ̄ⲙϵ ⲏⲗ[- - -]

    [- - -] . ⲣⲁ ⲅⲟⲗⲁ ϵιⲛ̄ⲛ̄[- - -]

10   [- - -]ⲗⲁ ⲟⲩⲇⲁϵ[- - -]

    [- - -]κⲁ . . . [- - -]

12   [- - -] . ϵⲗⲟ . [- - -]

    [- - -]λ̄ . . [- - -]

14   [- - -]ϵⲛ[- - -]

And Jesus Christ is [...] be in [...] giving to [...] we/you wish [...] with them [...].

Gospel of Matthew, [*Ammonian Section*] 49 [...]
(Mt. 6:25) [...] gulp/eat [...] and you (pl.) [...]

$\overline{\text{oz}}$: 77

1 ⲓⲥ ⲭⲥⲗⲗⲉ: "Jesus Christ" written as nomen sacrum and followed by determiner -ⲗ and conjunction -ⲗⲉ. The khi and sigma of ⲭ(ⲡⲓⲥⲧⲟ)ⲥ with an extended supralinear stroke are distinguishable, as well as perhaps the *iota* and *sigma* of ⲓ(ⲏⲥⲟⲩ)ⲥ.

   ⲉⲓⲛ̅-: perhaps a form of the copula ⲉⲓⲛ "to be" (ond 69).

3 -ⲛ̅ⲅⲟⲩⲗⲁ: possibly ending in plural -ⲅⲟⲩ and dative -ⲗⲁ.

   ⲗⲟⲩⲗⲗ-: probably a participial form of the existential verb ⲗⲟⲩ(ⲗ) "to be, exist," which has been attested with dative: M. 1.7 ⲗⲡ̄ⲡⲟⲩ ⲟⲩⲉⲗⲗⲁ ⲗⲟⲩⲁ̄ⲣⲁ.

4]ⲟⲩⲕⲁ: either ending in plural -ⲅⲟⲩ or exclusive first plural personal pronoun with accusative -ⲕⲁ, object of 4 ⲧ̄ⲟ̣ⲟ̣ⲁ̣, which suggests a plural (in)direct object.

   ⲧ̄ⲟ̣ⲟ̣ⲁ̣: ⲧⲣ̄ "to give (to s.o.)" (ond 174), with pluractional -ⲟ̄ and predicative -ⲁ.

5 ⲗⲟⲗⲗⲓⲣⲟ: ⲗⲟⲗⲗ "to wish, love" with first/second person plural present tense, followed by predicative -ⲁ, ⲗⲟⲗⲗⲓⲣⲟⲩ + -ⲁ > ⲗⲟⲗⲗⲓⲣⲟ.

6 ⲧⲉ̣ⲗⲗⲁⲗ: third person plural pronoun ⲧⲉⲣ followed by comitative -ⲗⲁⲗ.

7 ⲉⲩ̄: abbreviation of εὐαγγέλιον "Gospel"

   ⲙⲁⲑ: abbreviation for the Apostle's name Matthew.

   ⲙ[ⲑ: Ammonian Section 49, alias Mt 6:25–34 (see General Introduction, pp. 21–22).

9 ⲅⲟⲗⲁ: ⲅⲟⲗ- "to gulp" (ond 201), with predicative -ⲁ.

   ⲉⲓⲛ̅ⲛ-: perhaps a form of the copula ⲉⲓⲛ "to be." Cf. 1 ⲉⲓⲛ̅-.

10 ⲟⲩⲗⲗⲉ: perhaps a form of the second person plural pronoun.

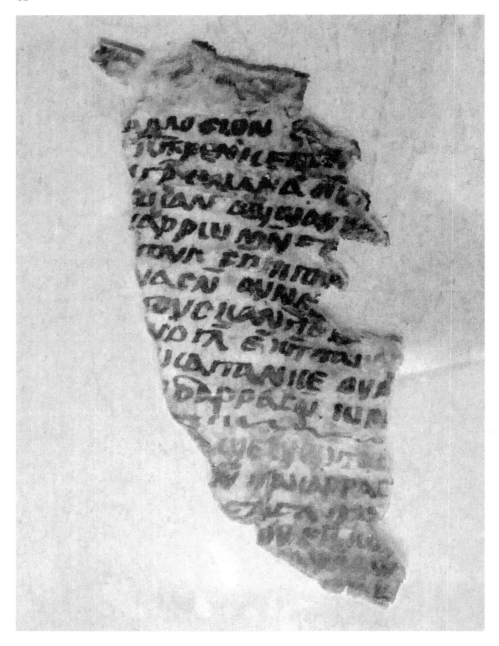

Fig. 6. P. Attiri 3.ii (SNM 23045). Photo by Vincent W.J. van Gerven Oei.

P. Attiri 3 (SNM 23045, ±5×10 cm)
ii – flesh side

```
         [ⲟ̄ⲏ̄]
     [- - -]ⲁⲗⲗⲟⲉⲓⲟⲛ ⲉ̣[- - -]
2    [- - -]ⲕⲧ̄ⲣⲉⲛⲕⲉⲧⲁ̣[ⲗⲗⲉ · ]
     [- - -] . ⲅⲣ̣ⲉ̣ⲛⲁⲛⲁ̄ ⲡⲅ̣ⲧ̣[ⲉⲩ - -]
4    [- - ⲙ]ⲁ̣ⲕⲁⲛ ⲁⲱ̣ⲱ̣ⲁⲩⲕ̣[ⲁⲧⲁⲛⲕⲉ - -]
     [- - -] . ⲁⲣⲣⲱ ⲙⲛ̄ ⲅ̣ⲉ̣[- - -]
6    [- - -]ⲅⲟⲩⲗ ⲥⲡ̄ⲡⲓ̣ⲅⲟⲩⲗ[- - -]
     [- - -]ⲛⲁⲥⲛ̄ ⲟⲩⲛⲛ̣[- - -]
8    [- - -]ⲧⲟⲩⲥⲕⲁⲛⲧⲉⲗ[ⲟ - -]
     [- - ⲟ]ⲩⲣⲅⲗ̄ ⲉ̄ⲕⲧ̄ⲧⲁⲕⲁⲣ[ⲣⲁ · ]
10   [- -ⲙⲁⲕⲁⲛ ⲁⲱ̣ⲱⲁⲩ]ⲕⲁⲧⲁⲛⲕⲉ ⲟⲩⲁ̣[- - -]
     [- - -] . ⲟ̄ⲁⲣⲣⲁⲥⲛ̄ ⲱⲣ . [- - -]
12   /////////////////////////////////////
     [- - -] ⲱ̣ⲉ̣ⲱ̣ⲟ̣ⲓⲧⲁⲛ̣[- - -]
14   [- - -]ⲛ̄ ⲧⲁⲕⲁⲣⲣⲁⲥ[ⲛ̄ - -]
     [- - -]ⲅ̣ⲁⲅ̣ⲁ ⲧ . [- - -]
16   [- - -]ⲟⲩⲉ̣ⲕ̣ⲕⲟ̣ . [- - -]
     [- - -] . ⲁ̣ⲯⲗ̄ⲗⲱ[- - -]
18   [- - -]
```

(Mt 6:30) [...] and [to morrow is cast into the oven, shall he not [much more clothe [you, O ye of little] faith?

(31) Therefore take no thought, [saying, What] shall we [eat? or,] What [shall we] drink? [or, Wherewithal shall we be clothed?]

(32) [(For] after all these things [do] the Gentiles [seek:)] for your [heavenly Father knoweth that ye have need of all these things.]

(33) [But seek ye] first [the kingdom of God, and his righteousness; and all these things shall] be added unto you.

(34) Take therefore no thought [for the morrow:] for [the morrow] shall take [...]

[...] *Sixty times/of sixty* [...]
[...] that will be covered [...]

The Old Nubian Texts from Attiri

[ⲟⲏ]: 78

1 -ⲁⲗⲗⲟⲉⲓⲟⲛ: ending in a locative or focus marker -ⲗⲟ and complementizer -ⲉⲓⲟⲛ.

2 ⲕⲧⲣⲉⲛⲕⲉⲧⲁ[ⲗⲗⲉ: ⲕⲓⲧ "to put on oneself" (OND 94) with transitive
   suffix -ⲡ "to dress someone" and third person singular present
   tense ending -ⲉⲛ suggesting a subordinate clause, followed by
   the -ⲕⲉⲧⲁⲗⲗⲉ "also." Cf. P. QI I 4.ii.11–12 ⲇⲓⲉⲛⲕⲉⲧⲁⲗ "even if he
   dies."

3 -ⲅⲣⲉⲛⲁⲛⲇ: either a verbal form with causative -ⲅⲡ̄ or an unknown
   adverb with -ⲅⲡ̄ meaning "rather" or "much more."
      ⲡ̣ⲥ̣ⲧ[ⲉⲩ: Greek loanword ⲡⲥ̄ⲧⲉⲩ(ⲉⲓ) "to believe" (OND 153).

4 ⲙ]ⲁ̣ⲕⲁⲛ: ⲙⲁⲕⲁⲛ "therefore" (OND 109). The only letter attested to
   appear before the sequence ⲁⲕⲁⲛ is *mu*.
      ⲁϣϣⲁⲩⲕ[ⲁⲧⲁⲛⲕⲉ: form of the verb ⲁϣϣⲁⲩⲉⲓ "to fear, worry"
   (OND 21), followed by habitual suffix -ⲕ and second person plural
   vetitive -ⲧⲁⲛⲕⲉ. The reconstruction is based on the repetition of
   the same phrase in 9, in both cases translating the Greek μὴ οὖν
   μεριμνήσητε (see General Introduction, p. 21). Cf. 1.ii.20 ⲁϣϣⲁ[.

5 -ⲁⲣⲣⲱ: verb form with the intentional suffix -ⲁⲇ followed by
   first/second person plural present tense with predicative -ⲣⲱ.
      ⲙⲛ̄: question word ⲙⲛ̄ (OND 117).
      ⲅ̣ⲉ̣-: ⲅⲉ(ⲓ) "to drink" (OND 200).

6 -ⲅⲟⲩⲗ: plural suffix -ⲅⲟⲩ followed by determiner -ⲗ. Perhaps to
   be reconstructed as ⲙⲟ̄ϣⲁⲛ]ⲅⲟⲩⲗ or ⲉⲓⲛⲛ̄]ⲅⲟⲩⲗ.
      ⲥⲛ̄ⲡ̣ⲓⲅⲟⲩ-: ⲥⲛ̄ⲡ- "nation" (OND 159) with plural -ⲅⲟⲩ and deter-
   miner -ⲗ, here used in the meaning of "Gentile."

7 -ⲛ̣ⲁⲥⲛ̄: noun or verb with emphatic suffix -ⲥⲛ̄.
      ⲟⲩⲛⲛ̣-: genitive of a second person plural pronoun, cf. 9
   ⲟ]ⲩⲡⲅⲗ̄.

8 ⲧⲟⲩⲥⲕⲁⲛⲧⲉ̣ⲗ[ⲟ: ⲧⲟⲩⲥⲕⲁⲛⲧⲉ(ⲗⲟ) "(at) first" (OND 184).

9 ⲟ]ⲩⲡⲅⲗ̄: second person plural pronoun ⲟⲩⲡ- with directive -ⲅⲗ̄.
   There is a second red stroke above the *lambda*,
      ⲉⲕⲧ̄ⲧⲁⲕⲁⲣ[ⲣⲁ]-: ⲉⲕ(ⲕ)- "to bring" (OND 66), with transitive -ⲓⲡ
   and passive -ⲧⲁⲕ, followed by preterite 1 -ⲁⲣ and reconstructed
   intentional -ⲡ and predicative.
      ⲁϣϣⲁⲩ]ⲕⲁⲧⲁⲛⲕⲉ: reconstructed based on the same phrase in
   4, ending in the second person plural vetitive -ⲧⲁⲛⲕⲉ.

10 -ⲇⲁⲣⲣⲁⲥⲛ̄: verbal form ending in pluractional -ⲇ, intentional
   -ⲁⲇ, present/neutral tense -ⲡ, and predicative -ⲁ (what Browne
   calls a "future predicative," ONG §3.9.6), followed by emphatic
   marker -ⲥⲛ̄.

13 ϣⲉϣϣⲓⲧⲁⲛ: possibly a form of a Ge'ez loanword meaning "sixty"
   (see General Introduction, p. 24)

14 ⲧⲁⲕⲁⲣⲣⲁⲥ̣[ⲛ̄: perhaps a form of ⲧⲁⲕ- "to be covered" (ⲟⲛⲇ 163)
    with intentional -ⲁⲗ, present/neutral -ⲣ, predicative -ⲁ, fol-
    lowed by emphatic -ⲥⲛ̄. Cf. 11] . ⳝⲁⲣⲣⲁⲥⲛ̄.
15 -ⲣ̣ⲁⳠⲁ: perhaps a verbal form ending in inchoative -ⲁⳠ and pred-
    icative -ⲁ.
16 ⲟⲩⲉ̱ⲕ̄ⲕ̣ⲟ-: perhaps an adjectival form of ⲟⲩⲉⲗ̄- "second" (ⲟⲛⲇ 134)
    with ⲕⲟⲛ "to have" or a verbal form of ⲟⲩⲉⲕⲕ "to throw" (ⲟⲛⲇ
    132).
17 -ⲁ̣ⲯⲗ̄ⲗⲱ: unknown nominal form, perhaps simply ⲁⲯ "to live"
    (ⲟⲛⲇ 23), ending in determiner -ⲗ and locative or focus marker
    -ⲗⲱ.

Fig. 7. P. Attiri 4.i (SNM 23045). Photo by Alexandros Tsakos.

P. Attiri 4 (SNM 23045, ±7×18 cm)
i – hair side

The two fragments with the same find no. are united in the transcription, because the straight cut of the two pieces produces a continuous reading if joined together using the red lines in each as a guide. Further proof of the unity of these two fragments is given by matching smudges in the writing as well as the overall consistency of the writing.

The line of separation is marked with [] in the transcription.

±3 lines
4 [- - -] . ṇ . [- - -]
   [- - -]ⲁ̣ⲛⲛ̣[] . . [- - -]
6 [- - - ο]ⲩⲕ[]ⲛ̄ ⲧⲁ[1–2]
   [- - -] . . []ⲟⲩⲛⲁ ·
8 [- - -] . . []ⲥ . . ⲉ̣
   [- - -] . . [] . . ⲛ̣ⲓⲁ
10 [- - -] . . []ⲛ̣ⲁ̣ⲗⲟ̣ . .
line with decoration
12 [- - -] . . ⲁ̣ⲡ̣ⲥ̣
   [- - -] ⲛ̣ .[] . . . ⲙⲁ̣
14 [- - -] ⲛ̣ . []
± 2 lines
   [- - -] . . ⲧⲁⲕⲁ
18 [- - -] . ⲁⲣⲟ̣ⲩ ⲧⲁ̣ⲩⲗⲗⲁ̄ⲱ̄
   [- - -]ⲁ̣ⲥⲱ ⲕⲟ̣ⲩⲣⲁⲫⲉ
20 [- - -] . ⲕⲁⲥ̄ⲛ̄ ⲡⲁ̣ ⲕⲉⲛ̣ .
   [- - -] . . . . ⲁ· ⲉ̄ⲣ̣ⲁ̣ . . [2–3]

[...]

[...] *Apostle*(?)
(2 Cor 12) [...] deceit [...] brother [...]

12   ⲁ̣ⲡⲥ̣: perhaps to be read as ⲁⲡ<ⲟ>ⲥ[ⲧⲟⲗⲟⲥ, cf. 4.ii.8 ⲧⲗⲟ`ⲧ´ⲥ̣: This
     reading seems to be confirmed by the fact that the text below
     can be identified with a section from Paul's Second Letter to the
     Corinthians (see General Introduction, p. 22).

18   ⲧ̣ⲁ̣ⲩⲗⲗⲱ̄: unknown word ending in locative or focus marker -ⲗⲱ.

19   -ⲁ̣ⲥ̣ⲱ: the end of an imperative form, either a second/third per-
     son plural or predicative -ⲁ followed by -ⲥⲱ.

     ⲕ̣ⲟ̣ⲩⲣⲁⲫⲉ: ⲕⲟⲩⲣⲁⲫⲉ "deceit" (OND 102).

20   ⲉ̄ⲣ̣ⲁ̣-: ⲉⲣⲣⲁⲗ "brother" (OND 62).

Fig. 8. P. Attiri 4.ii (SNM 23045). Photo by Alexandros Tsakos.

P. Attiri 4 (snm 23045, ±7×18 cm)
ii – flesh side

```
   [- - -]ελ[- - -]
2  [- - -]ΓΟΡ[- - -]
   [- - -]αλε[- - -]
4  [- - -]ΟΥΡ[- - -]
   ει[]ΨTT[- - -]
6  κε[]ταλ[- - -]
   ν`τ´ ΗC . [1–2]κΥ`κ´: . [- - -]
8  ΤλΟ`Τ´C[]ακε . [- - -]
   ΑΗΟΥ[]ëΜ[- - -]
10 πλερ[]ραδ[- - -]
   εÑΝα[]Να · [- - -]
12 ααλεΝ[]ΟΥ π[- - -]
   αΨοιϖ[] · ΟΥΤρ[- - -]
14 ΤΟκελλΟ[1–2]Οκκα[- - -]
   αΓΟΥλΟ εΝ[]ÑΓΟ[Υ - - -]
16 ΤικÑ κ̄ΤΤι[]κα[- - -]
   ΓαΥē ειΝλ̄ · Τε . [- - -]
18 ϲϢ οͦΥλλēλα[- - -]
   ΗϲαΛ ΟΥēλα εΝ . [- - -]
20 ΜεΝΝαΝαλΟ · ε . [- - - α]
   Μ̄Ϣ̄ϢαΝαε κΟϲ[- - -]
22 [- - -]
```

l. 8: alternative reading ΤλΟϲ̄

[...] commit [...] and also [...].

Fast; Sunday [...] *Apostle(?)* [...]
begging [...] they are [...] and [...] in the Savior/life [...] forgiving [...]
these [...] garment of [...] are [...] they are not [...] and all [...]

5   ει[]ψт̄т-: perhaps from ϥ̄ψ "to take, suffer, commit(?)" (ΟΝD 26)
     with nominalizer -т̄т. The meaning ειψт̄т "wealth" seems less
     likely.

6   -κε[]ταλ: -κεταλ "also" (ΟΝD 89).

7   ν`т´ нϲ . [1–2]κγ`κ´: . : abbreviations for Greek loanwords
     ннϲτεια "fast" and κγριακн "Sunday," cf. P. QI 1.i.4 ннϲ`т´ :
     κγρια`κ´. These abbreviations allow the identification of this
     text of this manuscript as a lectionary, of this line as the incipit
     to the reading suggested, and of the text that follows as the bib-
     lical passage to be read during Mass in that Sunday of the Lent
     (see General Introduction, p. 22).

8   ταο`т´ϲ: perhaps to be read as αποϲ]т<ο>λοϲ, which identifies
     this as a reading from the Pauline Epistles (see General Intro-
     duction, p. 22).

9   ληογ: perhaps from λι-/λει- "to die" (ΟΝD 44).

10   πιλερ[]ραλ-: unattested verb πιλ-ερ-, possibly related to Ν *fedd*
     "betteln, ersuchen," (Khalil 113) and D *bedd* "to pray, beg, en-
     treat" (Armbruster 31) with transitive suffix -ερ present tense -ρ
     with predicative -α, the -λ- could be part of the next word.

11   εν̄να[]να: ειν "to be" (ΟΝD 69), with third person plural present
     tense + predicative -ανα.

12   αλλεν[]ογ: ending in conjunction -λενογ "and" (ΟΝD 41).

13   αψοῖω̄: αψοῖ "life, savior" (ΟΝD 23), with locative -ω.
         ογтρ-: root of the verb ογтρ "put, hold" (ΟΝD 141).

14   тοκελλο: possibly participial form of тοκ "to forgive," (ΟΝD 177)
     with present tense/determiner -ελ and locative or focus marker
     -λο.

15   αρογλο: ending in plural -ρογ and locative or focus -λο.
         εν[]ν̄ρο[γ: proximate determinative plural pronoun.

16   тικν̄: possibly a noun ending in genitive -ν̄.
         κ̄т̄τι[]κα: κιтт "garment" (ΟΝD 94), with accusative -κα.

17   ραγε̄: Not attested as the ending of any known ON word. The
     ending -αγε̄ appears only on the nominalizer -ναγε̄.
         εινλ̄: ειν "to be," with determiner λ̄.

18   -ϲω: the end of an imperative form.
         ǒογλλελα: complex verb perhaps consisting of the unattested
     verb ǒογλλ followed by ελ "to find" (ΟΝD 56) and predicative -α.

19   ογελα: perhaps from ογε "to say" (ΟΝD 204).

20   μεννanalo: from negative verb μεν (ΟΝD 114) with third person
     plural present tense plus predicative -ανα, followed by focus
     marker -λο.

21   μⲧ̄ϣανλε: μⲧ̄ϣαν "all" (ΟΝD 118) with conjunction -λε.

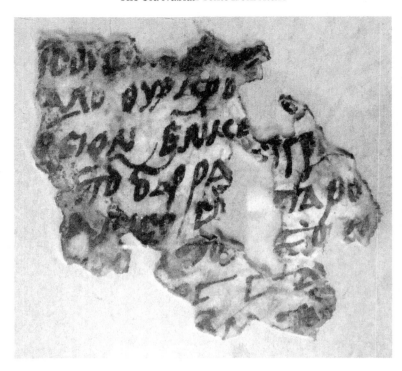

Fig. 9. P. Attiri 5.i (ѕɴм 23045). Photo by Vincent W.J. van Gerven Oei.

P. Attiri 5
Unidentified fragment

An unidentified parchment fragment from the middle of a page. It preserves 8 lines of text that are written with black ink in Nubian majuscules.

P. Attiri 5 (SNM 23045, ±7×7 cm)
i – flesh side

```
   [- - -]ιϲογ . κα̣[- - -]
2  [- - -] . αλο ογρκρο . [- - -]
   [- - -] . ειον ε̄ν̄κε̣ [1–2] . [- - -]
4  [- - -]τ̄οδαρρα [1]ιг̣ρ̣α̣[- - -]
   [- - -]ακιϲο cῑ̄[ni] ταρο[γ- - -]
6  [- - -] . . . . τογ [1] го[γ]ν̣[- - -]
   [- - -]ε̂гга . [- - -]
8  [- - -]λ̄λ̣α τα̣ọ[- - -]
```

[...] we/you are hungry [...]. And [...] will give (them) [...] we remained(?) blessed nations [...] brother [...]

1 -ιϲογ: possibly the ending of a Greek loanword.
2 -αλο: possibly an ending in predicative -α and focus marker -λο.
   ογρκρο: ογρκ "to be hungry," cf. 2.ii.2, 14, with present tense first/second plural predicative -ρο.
3 -ειον: complementizer -ειον, beginning of a new sentence.
4 τ̄οδαρρα: full verb form of τρ̄ "to give," with pluractional -ϭ, intentional -αλ, present tense -ρ, and predicative -α.
   -ιг̣ρ̣α̣-: perhaps a verbal form with causative -ιгρ.
5 ακιϲο: if this is an entire verb form, it may be ακ "to sit, remain" (OND 8) with preterite 2 -ιϲ and first/second person plural and predicative -ο.
   cῑ̄[ni]: probably cῑ̄ni "nation, people," (OND 159).
   ταρο[γ-: possibly ταρογ(ογ) "to bless, praise" (OND 167).
6 гο[γ]ν̣-: beginning of an unknown word.
7 ε̂гга-: possibly εггαλ "brother" (OND 62).
8 -λ̄λ̣α: possibly a determiner followed by a dative ending in -λ̄-λα.
   τα̣ọ-: if the preceding word ends in a dative then perhaps a form of ταϭ "to call" (OND 168).

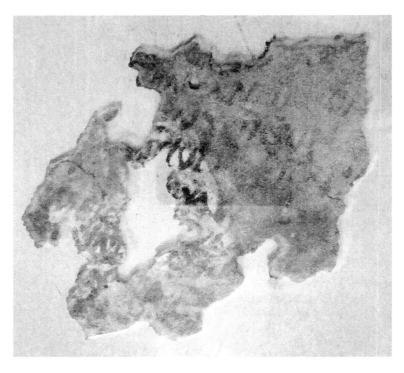

Fig. 10. P. Attiri 5.ii (SNM 23045). Photo by Vincent W.J. van Gerven Oei.

P. Attiri 5 (SNM 23045, ±7×7 cm)
ii – hair side

```
   [- - -]
2  [- - -]. ⲗ . ⲁⲗⲡⲓⲕ[- - -]
   [- - -]ⲉ̣ⲛ . . ⲧⲕ̄ⲕⲓⲛ[- - -]
4  [- - -]ⲁⲡⲟⲓ̣[- - -]
   [- - -]ⲁ̇ⲩⲁ[- - -]
6  [- - -]ⲙⲉⲕ [4–5] ⲩⲗⲗ[- - -]
   [- - -]ⲁ̇ⲧⲟ̣ⲥ [1–2] ⲕ̄[- - -]
8  [- - -]ⲉ̣ⲯ . . ⲁ · ⲣ̣ⲁ̇ [- - -]
   [- - -]ⲉ̣[- - -]
```

7   -ⲁ̇ⲧⲟ̣ⲥ: perhaps a part of a Greek loanword.
8   ⲣ̣ⲁ-: there are a variety of ON words starting with ⲣⲁ-. Owing to
    a lack of context an educated guess is out of the question.

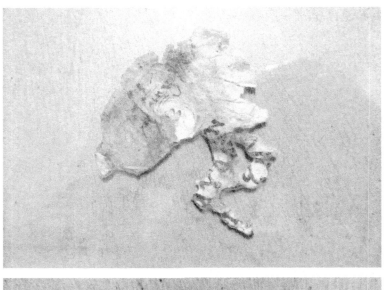

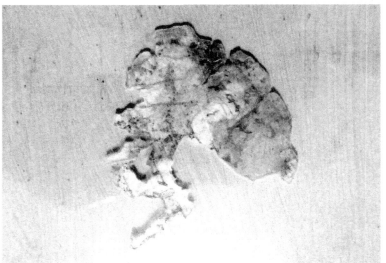

Fig. 11. P. Attiri 6.i (SNM 23045). Photo by Vincent W.J. van Gerven Oei.
Fig. 12. P. Attiri 6.ii (SNM 23045). Photo by Vincent W.J. van Gerven Oei.

P. Attiri 6
Fragment

A scrap of parchment with traces of writing in black ink on both sides. There are two distinctive scripts, a smaller one written on the upper margin of the flesh side, which appear to be traces of a scribe trying out his pen,[1] and a larger one both on the flesh and the hair side, which paleographically appears more like a Coptic majuscule than Old Nubian, owing to the absence of a distinctly slanted appearance. Also the suspected presence of a *hori* with a closed upper loop in line 3 suggests Coptic. Apart from the lines of trial characters and lines, we can discern four lines of Coptic/Old Nubian on the flesh side. The hair side has three.

---

1   We thank Willem Flinterman for this insight.

P. Attiri 6 (SNM 23045, ±5.5×5 cm)
i – flesh side

> [- - -]ɴ[- - -]
> 2   [- - ϭ]ⲁⲩⲟɴ[- - -]
> [- - -] ! [1–2] ⲌⲈ[- - -]
> 4   [- - -]

2   ϭ]ⲁⲩⲟɴ: if indeed the text is in Coptic, the only plausible reconstruction seems to be ϭ]ⲁⲩⲟɴ "servant" (CRUM, *A Coptic Dictionary*, 835).

3   ⲌⲈ: if this reading is correct and the text is Coptic then the only combination of these two letters in a single word is the verb ⲋⲁⲌⲟⲈ "to fight" (CRUM, *A Coptic Dictionary*, 839).

ii – hair side

> ⲧ[- - -]
> 2   . ⲧⲀⲧ[- - -]
> . [- - -]

Fig. 13.　P. Attiri 7.A–B–C, side 1 (SNM 23045). Photo by Alexandros Tsakos.
Fig. 14.　P. Attiri 7.B–A–C, side 2 (SNM 23045). Photo by Alexandros Tsakos.

P. Attiri 7
Fragments

Three fragments of parchment: fragment A has a triangular shape, with sides of approx. 2 cm with writing on side one; fragment B has a square shape, with sides of approx. 2 cm with writing on side two; fragment C has a rectangular shape, measuring about 1.5 × 4 cm, containing no discernible writing.

P. Attiri 7 (SNM 23045)
A, side 1 (2×2 cm)

   [- - -]ϵⲚⲞⲚ[- - -]
2 [- - -]ⲇⲟⲩⲇ[- - -]
   [- - -] . . [- - -]

1   -ϵⲚⲞⲚ-: possibly part of a verbal form.
2   ⲇⲟⲩⲇ-: possibly a verbal form of ⲇⲟⲩⲇ-ⲡ̄ "to go, proceed" (OND 194).

B, side 2 (2×2 cm)

   [- - -]ⲁ̣ⲓ̣[- - -]
2 [- - -] . ⲁⲩ[- - -]
   [- - -] . . ⲓ̣ⲥⲁ̣[- - -]

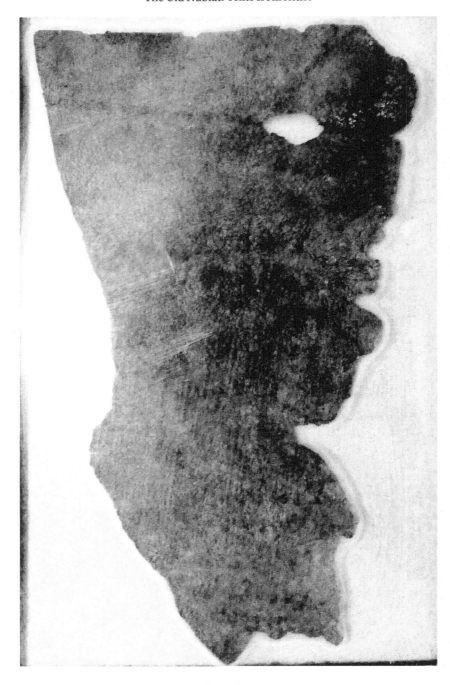

Fig. 15. P. Attiri 8 (SNM 23047). Photo by Alexandros Tsakos.

P. Attiri 8
The Head

SNM 23047

Very dark leather fragment of approx. 13×22.5 cm with a small hole towards the top. No text is immediately visible on Side A, but visible text on Side B suggests the existence of a single line at the top with about one line of white space, followed by thirteen lines of written text. Enhanced photographic techniques would be necessary to bring the contents of this document to light. For a discussion of its shape, see General Introduction, p. 25.

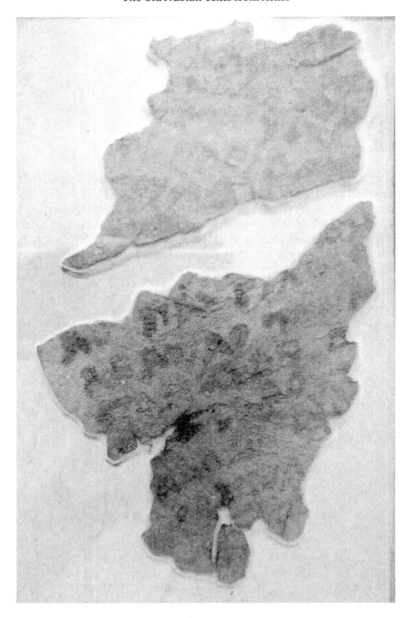

Fig.16.   P. Attiri 9.B, 9.A (SNM 23047). Photo by Vincent W.J. van Gerven Oei.

P. Attiri 9
Sale

Two fragments of leather inscribed only on the hair side, which at its present state preserves 12–13 lines of text. The fragment on the upper side of the photo preserves the lower margin of the writing surface and so it appears second in the transcription. Both fragments are written in the same hand and apparently belong to the same document.

P. Attiri 9 (SNM 23047)
A, lower fragment (9×10 cm)

```
    [4–5] ⲣ [4–5] . ⲟ̣ⲛ̣ [- - -]
2   ⲗⲟ ⲡⲁ[ⲡ]ϭ̣ⲓⲗ̣ⲟ̣ ⲧ̣[- - -]
    ⲗⲉⲙⲓⲗⲟ ⲧⲁⲛⲛ̣[- - -]
4   ⲧⲁⲡⲗ̄ⲗⲟ̣ⲛ . [- - -]
    ⲧⲁ̣ⲉ̄ⲥⲁⲗⲟ . [- - -]
6   ⲕⲟⲁ̣ⲗⲟ ⲁ̈ⲟ̣ⲩ[- - -]
    ϭ̣ⲉ̣[ⲛ]ⲧⲟⲗ[- - -]
8   ⲟ̣ⲩ . ⲧ̣ . [- - -]
```

[...] bishop [...] -lem [...] and his father [...] name [...] I [...] request [...]

B, upper fragment (8×5 cm)

```
    [- - -]ⲉ̣ [1–2] ⲗⲟ [- - -]
2   [- - -] . ⲥⲗ̄ⲗⲟ̣ ⲧⲣⲣ . [- - -]
    [- - -]ⲉⲛⲁⲉⲓ ⲙ̣ . [- - -]
4   [- - -] . ⲙⲱⲩⲥⲏ . [- - -]
    [- - -]ⲟ̣ⲛ ⲡⲁⲉⲓⲥⲉⲗ[ⲟ - - -]
6   [- - -]ⲧⲟⲩⲥⲕⲗ̄ . [- - -]
```

[...] Mōusē [...] I have written [and witnessed] [...] *touski* [...]

A

2 ⲡⲁ[ⲡ]ϭⲓⲗⲟ: possibly ⲡⲁⲡⲥ̄ "bishop, father" (OND 145), with focus
   marker -ⲗⲟ.

3 -ⲗⲉⲙⲓⲗⲟ: if analyzed as a noun marked with a locative -ⲗⲟ, only
   ⲃⲏⲑⲗⲉ̄ⲙⲏ "Bethlehem," or a previously unattested variant spelling of ïⲉ̄ⲣⲟⲩⲥⲁⲗ(ⲏ)ⲙⲏ "Jerusalem" would be possible here. Considering that this a land sale in Nubia, these readings seem very
   unlikely. Alternatively, it may be another personal name with
   focus marker -ⲗⲟ.

4 ⲧⲁⲡⲗ̄ⲗⲟⲛ: possibly ⲧⲁⲡ "his father," cf. 1.ii.7 ⲧⲁ̣ⲡⲡⲁⲕⲁ, with determiner -ⲗ̄ and conjunction -ⲗⲟⲛ.

5 ⲧⲁ̣ⲣ̄ⲥⲁⲗⲟ: ⲧⲁⲣ̄ⲥ̄ "name" (OND 168), with predicative -ⲁ and focus
   marker -ⲗⲟ.

6 -ⲕ̣ⲟⲁ̣ⲗⲟ: verbal form ending in predicative -ⲁ and focus marker
   -ⲗⲟ.

   ⲁïⲟ̣ⲩ: first person singular pronoun.

7 ϭⲉ̣[ⲛ]ⲧⲟⲗ: probably ϭⲉⲛⲧⲟⲗ, related to ϭⲉⲛⲧ "request" (OND 157).

B

2 -ⲥⲗ̄ⲗⲟ̣: the end of a preterite 2 participial form with -ⲥ, determiner -ⲗ̄, and focus or locative marker -ⲗⲟ.

   ⲧ̣ⲣⲣ: perhaps a form of ⲧⲣ̄ "to give."

4 ⲙⲱⲩⲥⲏ: proper name "Mōusē/Moses."

5 ⲡⲁⲉⲓⲥⲉⲗ[ⲟ: ⲡⲁⲣ "to write" (OND 145) with preterite 2 -ⲥ and first
   person singular followed by predicative -ⲉ and focus marker
   -ⲗⲟ. Considering the type of text, we would expect a verbal form
   with noun ⲙⲁⲧⲁⲣ "witness" (OND 112) (see General Introduction,
   pp. 25–26).

6 ⲧⲟⲩⲥⲕⲗ̄: possibly ⲧⲟⲩⲥⲕ "kind of food or beverage" (OND 183) with
   determiner -ⲗ̄, cf. P. QI 3 32.26 ⲧⲟⲩⲥⲕⲗ̄ ⲅ̄·ⲕⲟ (with note *ad loc.*); P.
   QI 4 69.24 ⲧⲟⲩⲥⲕⲏ ϥ̄·; Nauri 11 ⲧⲟⲩϭⲓ ⲝⲝ̄ : ⲉⲗⲟ.[1] This is presumably
   (part of) the tariff for the witnesses or the scribe.[2]

---

1 Browne's lemma in OND is ⲧⲟⲩⲥⲕⲗ̄, but the attestation in P. QI 4 of the form ⲧⲟⲩⲥⲕⲏ shows that
   the final -ⲗ̄ should be interpreted as a determiner and not part of the stem.
2 See RUFFINI, *Medieval Nubia*, pp. 116–19.

Fig. 17. P. Attiri 10 (SNM 23047). Photo by Vincent W.J. van Gerven Oei.

P. Attiri 10
Unidentified document

Very dark piece of leather of approx. 8 × 12 cm, with text on flesh side. The leather sheet has been inscribed in two different orientations, with the change noted between lines 4 and 5. There are two large ink blots on line 3 and one on line 4.

P. Attiri 10 (SNM 23047, ±8×12 cm)

In one orientation, tilted upward:

    [- - -]ⲧ . ⲟⲧ[- - -]
2   [- - -]ⲁ ⲁ̅ⲕⲕⲟⲕ[- - -]
    [- - -] ̣ · ⲗ̅ · ⲗⲟ ⲛ[- - -]
4   [- - -]. . ⲕⲟⲗ· ⲉ[- - -]

In another orientation, tilted downward:

    [- - ⲙ]ⲁ ̣ⲱⲉ · ⳝ · ⲗⲟ · [- - -]
6   [- - -]ⲗⲓⲥⲁ ̣ⲛ̣ⲛ̣[ⲟ - - -]
    [- - -]ⲧⲁ · ⲟⲣⲡⲉⲕ ̣ⲁ
8   [- - -]ⲧⲛ̅ ⲉⲓⲟⲩⲛ ⳝⲉⲣ
    [- - -] . ⲡ̅ⲥ̅ⲣ̅ · ⲏ̅ⲗⲟ ·
10   [- - -]

[...] who has remained [...] 4 [...] 6 measures [...] they -ed [...] wine [...] of grain [...] priest 8 [...]

2   ⲁ̄ⲕⲕⲟⲕ-: perhaps to be reconstructed as ⲁ̄ⲕⲕⲟⲕ[ⲕⲁ], from ⲁⲕ "to
     sit, remain" (OND 8) with preterite 1 -ⲟ, determiner -ⲗ (with re-
     gressive assimilation), and accusative -ⲕⲁ. This would suggest a
     relative clause construction.

3   ⲇ̄ · ⲗⲟ: number 4.

5   ⲙ]ⲁϣⲉ: ⲙⲁϣⲉ "measure" (OND 113).
     ⲋ · ⲗⲟ: number 6.

6   ]ⲗⲓⲥⲁ̣ⲛ̣ⲛ̣[ⲟ: probably a verbal form, ending in preterite 2 -ⲓⲥ, third
     person plural with focus marker -ⲗⲟ.

7   ⲟⲣⲡⲉⲕⲁ: ⲟⲣⲡ- "wine" (OND 128) with accusative -ⲉⲕⲁ.

8   ⲉⲓⲟⲩⲛ: ⲉⲓⲟⲩ- "grain" with genitive -ⲛ.
     ⲇ̃ⲉⲣ cannot be ⲇ̃ⲉⲣ "tribe" (OND 189) within this context. Per-
     haps a variant of ⲕⲉⲣ, ⲅⲉⲣ "to gather" (OND 89), cf. in P. QI 4
     94.5, meaning some "assembling" as a "sheaf" or a measure as
     a "bushel."

9   ⲡ̄ⲥ̄ⲣ̄ : Abreviation for Greek loanword ⲡⲣⲉⲥⲃⲩⲧⲉⲣ "priest."
     ⲏ̄ⲗⲟ: number 8.

Fig. 18. P. Attiri 11 (SNM 23049). Photo by Alexandros Tsakos.

P. Attiri 11
Letter

Single leather sheet, folded five times and inscribed on one side with 9 lines of a text written with black ink. Traces of ink on the other side too, but illegible.

P. Attiri 11 (SNM 23049, ±20×15 cm)

```
    + ⲇⲁⲩⲕⲟⲩⲙⲉⲗⲱ ⲉⲓⲁⲅⲣⲓⲙⲗⲱ · ⲡⲟⲩⲧⲟⲩ ⲙⲁⲱⲉ
2   ⲕⲉⲟⲩⲧ ⲕ̣ⲓⲇⲇⲓ · ⲏ̅ · ⲥⲓⲇⲗⲱ · ⲕⲉⲟⲩⲧ · ⲇ ·
    ⲥⲩⲕⲙⲓ · ⲉ̅ · ⲗⲱ · ⲥⲩⲣⲕⲓ · ⲙⲟⲣ · ⲇ · ⲟⲣⲡⲟⲩ · ⲏ̅ ·
4   ⲕ̣ⲟⲡⲁⲧⲟ̣ⲓ · ⲇ · ⲉⲕⲧⲟⲩ · ⲑ̅ · ⲧⲟⲗⲥⲟⲩ · ⲃ̅ · ⲙ̣ⲁⲧⲓ̣ⲥ̣ⲕ ·
    ⲅⲟⲩⲣⲣⲟⲩ · ⲏ̅ · ⲡⲁⲕⲓ · ⲇⲁⲇⲕⲁ · ⲕⲟⲩⲗⲱ ⲟⲣⲡⲟⲩ
6   · ⲃ̅ · ⲡⲁⲗⲁⲅⲉⲗⲁ · ⲁⲑⲓⲧⲓ · . ⲕⲁ ⲟⲣⲡⲟⲩ ⲟⲥⲕⲟⲩⲇⲁ
    ⲇⲓⲉⲓⲛⲕⲟⲩⲗⲁ · ⲡⲉ̣ⲧ̣ⲉ̣ · ⲕⲟⲩⲇ ⲇⲓⲉⲓⲛⲅⲟⲩⲗ[ⲁ]
8   ⲕⲓⲡⲓⲥⲕⲟ ⲕⲣⲉⲛⲟⲧⲟⲣⲁ̣ · ⲟⲣ̣ⲡⲟⲩ · ⲃ̅ · ⲉ̣ⲕⲧⲟⲩ . . .
    . . . . ⲥⲉ · ⲅ̣ⲁⲉⲓ ⲥⲁ̣ⲡⲓ ⲧⲟⲣⲁ̣ · ⲁⲣⲓ̣ⲗⲱ ⲕⲓⲣⲡⲁⲅⲟ̣ⲩ [1–2]
```

l. 1: the letter ⲙ in ⲙⲁⲱⲉ has been written over a letter ⲡ.
l. 2: between ⲧ and ⲕ in ⲕⲉⲟⲩⲧ ⲕⲓⲇⲇⲓ there can be seen traces of an ⲏ that was possibly written first and then corrected, since it is repeated right after ⲕⲓⲇⲇⲓ.

I pay homage (to you). I inform (you).
   (1) cubit measure of millet; 8 garments; 4 cubits of chaff; 5 round flat loaves; 4 artabs of unmatured dates; 8 (amphorae of) wine; 4 flat loaves; 9 sheep; 2 *tol*; 8 eastern(?) oxes; (1) goat.
   Having consumed wine with many (of the family of) Oskouda and dates with many (of the family of) Kouda he comes and deposits 2 (amphorae) of wine coming out (of) Attiri at the Dadka cave.
   The 2 (amphorae of) wine; [...] sheep.
   Who enters(?) the tail of the island [...] wages.

1   ⲇⲁⲩⲕⲟⲩⲙⲉⲗⲱ: "I pay homage (to you)." Standard opening greet-
ing of a letter, cf. P. QI 4 94.r.1 ⲇⲟⲩⲕⲙ̄ⲙⲉⲗⲟ. The specific spelling, with stem vowel/diphthong ⲁⲩ instead of ⲟⲩ and epenthetic
vowel ⲟⲩ instead of ⲓ (or supralinear stroke) has not been attested elsewhere. Although the latter can be explained as an
effect of vowel harmony (otherwise occasionally attested), the
variation ⲟⲩ/ⲁⲩ remains a hapax. Another uncommon feature is
the spelling -ⲙⲉ for -ⲙⲙⲉ, a haplography that is otherwise not attested. In short, the first word of this text signals an unfamiliar-
ity with standard ON letter-writing conventions.

   ⲉⲓⲁⲅⲣⲓⲙⲗⲱ: "I inform you." Another stock phrase of letters, cf.
P. QI 4 102.r.1–2 ⲉⲓ̈ⲁⲣ̄ⲗⲅ̄ⲣⲙ̄ⲙⲉⲗⲟ, P. QI 4 107.r.1–2 ⲉⲓⲁⲣ̄ⲗⲅⲉⲙⲙⲉⲗⲟ. Note
the shortening of the affirmative suffix -ⲙⲙⲉ to a single *mu*, cf. P.
QI 4 102.r.1 ⲇⲁⲟⲩⲙⲗⲟ.

   ⲡⲟⲩⲧⲟⲩ: possibly *poutti* "Hirse" (Khalil 93). For an explanation of the structure of the itemized list see the General Introduction, pp. 26–27.

   ⲙⲁϣⲉ: ⲙⲁϣⲉ- "measure, bushel" (ᴏɴᴅ 113).

2   ⲕⲉⲟⲩⲧ: ⲕⲉϫⲓ- "cubit" (ᴏɴᴅ 89), cf. P. QI 4 94.r.7 ⲕⲉϫⲓⲕⲁⲕⲁ, but with
unexplained final *tau*. We would also expect a number to follow,
cf. P. QI 3 30.20 ⲁⲡⲥⲓⲟⲛ· ⲕⲉⲟⲩ· ⲍ̄ⲕⲁ· "7 cubit of wormwood." Perhaps it is better to interpret 1–2 ⲡⲟⲩⲧⲟⲩ ⲙⲁϣⲉ ⲕⲉⲟⲩⲧ "one cubit
measure of millet."

   ⲕⲓⲇⲇⲓ: probably from ⲕⲧ̄ⲧ "garment" (ᴏɴᴅ 94). Note, however, that the ⲇ/ⲧ alternation is not well attested in ON (ᴏɴɢ 18). It
may be a different word altogether.

   ⲏ̄ · ⲥⲓⲇⲗⲱ: ⲏ̄ "8." We would expect immediately the focus
marker -ⲗⲱ to follow, but find the unexplained morpheme *sid-*.
We know from 6 ⲟⲥⲕⲟⲩⲇⲇ that the scribe sometimes spelled
numbers fully, but there is no known Old Nubian number that
would fit this sequence. The other option is that ⲥⲓⲇⲗⲱ is the
substance that there is 2 ⲕⲉⲟⲩⲧ · ⲇ "4 cubit" of. In that case, ⲥⲓⲇ
may be possibly related to N *sitti* "Spreu" (Reinisch 144) with focus marker -ⲗⲱ, even though comparative data show that the
correlation between ON -ⲇ and NKD -*tt* is not well attested.[1]

3   ⲥⲩⲕⲙⲓ: previously unattested noun but perhaps related to D *sug*
"round flat loaf" (Armbruster 181)

   ⲉ̄ · ⲗⲱ: ⲉ̄ "5." Note that in this list, it is the only item for which
a -ⲗⲱ follows the number.

   ⲥⲩⲣⲕⲓ: Probably an unattested product measured in 3 ⲙⲟⲣ "artab." Possibly related to N *širg* "faulen, schlecht werden (Eier);
anfangen zu reifen, gelb werden (Dattelernte)" (Khalil 125).

   ⲙⲟⲣ: measuring unit "artab" (ᴏɴᴅ 120).

_____

1   Rɪʟʟʏ, *Le méroïtique et sa famille linguistique*, p. 221.

ορπογ: Coptic loanword ορπ "wine" (OND 128).

4 ⳓⲟⲡⲁⲧⲟⲓ̈: possibly a composite noun, from ⲕⲁⲡⲡⲁ "loaf (of bread)" (OND 85) and unattested adjective perhaps related to *tajj* "abge-flacht" (Khalil 111).

ⲉⲕⲧⲟⲩ: unattested, possibly N *eged* "Schaf" (Reinisch 33). Note that SC 1.7 has ⲧⲓⲕⲁⲛ for "sheep," related to D *tīgañ*; in P. Attiri 3 we found the inverse situation with ⲟⲩⲣⲕ "to be hungry."

ⲧⲟⲗⲥⲟⲩ: unknown. Between "sheep" and "ox," it could be an-other animal.

ⲙⲁⲧⲓⳓⲕ: unattested, possibly related to ⲙⲁⲧⲧⲟ "east," designat-ing the type of 5 ⲅⲟⲩⲣⲣⲟⲩ.

5 ⲅⲟⲩⲣⲣⲟⲩ: unattested, probably related to N *gur* "Rind" (Reinisch 54).

ⲡⲁⲕⲓ: unattested, probably N *fag, faki*, "Ziege" (Reinisch 39).

ⲁⲁⲁⲕⲁ: it is attractive to interpret the -ⲕⲁ as accusative case, but there is no verb it could be an object of. As it seems to be followed by the noun 5 ⲕⲟⲩⲗⲱ "cave," it is perhaps the name of the cave, cf. attested names P. QI 3 34.i.18 ⲁⲁⲁⲥⲟⲩⲗ; P. QI 3 30.11 ⲁⲁⲕⲕⲟⲩⲗ.

ⲕⲟⲩⲗⲱ: perhaps ⲕⲟⲩⲗ "cave, mountain" (OND 101) with loctive -(ⲗ)ⲱ.

ορπογ: ορπ "wine," cf. 3 ορπογ.

6 ⲡⲁⲗⲁⳓⲉⲗⲁ: seems like a verbal form with ⲡⲁⲗ "to come out" (OND 143) and inchoative -ⲁⳓ. The ending -ⲉⲗⲁ is more difficult to anal-yse. If present tense + predicative, we would expect -ⲉⲣⲁ, and a participial form ending in dative -ⲗⲁ would have -ⲉⲗⲗⲁ. How-ever, we already have a case of haplography in 1 ⲁⲁⲩⲕⲟⲩⲙⲉⲗⲱ, so perhaps this is another one. The supposed subject of ⲡⲁⲗⲁⳓⲉⲗⲁ is the 2 amphora of wine.

ⲁⲟⲓⲧⲓ: possibly a place name, perhaps a variant of ⲁⲧⲧⲓⲣⲓ > ⲁⲧⲧⲓⲁⲓ (a relatively common orthographical variation), written as ⲁⲟⲓⲧⲓ (following the scribe's confusion between voiced and voiceless consonants, see General Introduction, p. 27).

. -ⲕⲁ: perhaps an accusative case attached to the entire pre-ceding noun phrase, object of 8 ⲕⲣⲉⲛⲟⲧⲟⲣⲁ

ορπογ: ορπ "wine," cf. 3, 5 ορπογ.

ⲟⲥⲕⲟⲩⲁⲁ: unknown element ⲟⲥ- with the onomastic element -ⲕⲟⲩⲁⲁ, cf. P. QI 2 24.4 ⲕⲟⲩⲁⲁ. Also cf. 7 ⲕⲟⲩⲁ.

7 ⲁⲓⲉⲓⲛⲕⲟⲩⲗⲁ: ⲁⲓⲉⲓ "to be many" (OND 45), with plural -ⲕⲟⲩ and dative -ⲗⲁ. The *nu* is probably the same as in P. QI 2 16.vii.4–5 ⲕⲉⲛⲥⲱⲛⲅⲟⲩⲕⲁ, and perhaps just the plural morpheme -ⲛ(ⲓ).

ⲡⲉⲧⲉ: ⲡⲉⲧⲓ "date, date palm" (OND 150).

ⲕⲟⲩⲗ: name Kouda, cf. 6 ⲟⲥⲕⲟⲩⲁⲁ.

ⲁⲓⲉⲓⲛⲅⲟⲩⲗ[ⲁ]: cf. 7 ⲁⲓⲉⲓⲛⲕⲟⲩⲗⲁ. We take both 6–7 ορπογ ⲟⲥⲕⲟⲩⲁⲁ.

ⲁⲓⲉⲓⲛⲕⲟⲩⲗⲁ and 7 ⲛⲉ̣ⲧⲉ̣ · ⲕⲟⲩⲁ ⲁⲓⲉⲓⲛⲅⲟⲩⲗ[ⲁ] to be dependent on 8 ⲕⲓⲡⲓⲥⲕⲟ.

8   ⲕⲓⲡⲓⲥⲕⲟ: appears to be an adjective in -ⲕⲟ with the verb ⲕⲓⲡ "to eat" (OND 84), perhaps with preterite 2 -ⲥ. Another option would be to treat this as some type of perfect participle, as -ⲕⲟ forms are known in modern Nubian languages. For -ⲓⲥⲕ also cf. 4 ⲙⲁⲧⲓ̣ⲥ̣ⲕ̣.

ⲕⲣⲉⲛⲟⲧⲟⲣⲁ̣: perhaps verb ⲕⲣ̄ "to come" (OND 91) with present tense second/third person singular ending, and ⲟⲧⲟⲣ, from ⲟⲩⲧⲟⲩⲣ "to deposit" (OND 141) with predicative -ⲁ: "you/he comes bringing." An object, however, seems to be completely absent.

ⲟ̣ⲣⲡⲟⲩ · ⲃ̄: maybe the same two amphorae previously mentioned.

ⲉ̣ⲕⲧⲟⲩ: cf. 4 ⲉⲕⲧⲟⲩ

9   -ⲥⲉ: possibly a preterite 2, first person singular "I have…" If this is a letter, we would expect ⲡⲁⲉⲓⲥⲉ "I have written" at this point.

ⲅ̣ⲁⲉⲓ: "who?" (OND 195).

ⲥⲁ̣ⲡⲓ: perhaps "enclosure" (OND 156), but this meaning is dubious, cf. P. QI 4 110.7 and comm. *ad loc.* According to Rilly, "plutôt 'partie en aval d'une île' (nobiin *sáab*, Werner, c.p.)."[2]

ⲧⲟⲣⲁ̣: possibly *tor* "hineingehen, eintreten" (Khalil 108) with predicative -ⲁ.

ⲁⲣⲓ̣ⲗ̣ⲱ: perhaps a participial form of ⲁⲣ "take" with present tense/determiner -ⲓⲗ and focus marker -(ⲗ)ⲱ.

ⲕⲓⲣⲡⲁⲅⲟⲩ: possibly ⲕⲟⲣⲡⲁ "(wages for?) work" (OND 99[3]) with plural ending -ⲅⲟⲩ.

---

2   RILLY, *Le méroïtique et sa famille linguistique*, p. 473.
3   See also RUFFINI, *Medieval Nubia*, p. 182.

Bibliography

ABDEL-HAFIZ, Ahmed Sokarno. *A Reference Grammar of Kunuz Nubian* [= *Dotawo Monographs* 2]. Earth: punctum books, forthcoming.

ADAMS, W. Y. "Islamic Archaeology in Nubia: An Introductory Survey." In *Nubian Culture Past and Present*, ed. T. Hägg. Stockholm, 1987: pp. 327–61.

ALCOCK, Anthony. "Two Fragments of the Acts of Andrew and Paul (Cod. Borg. Copt. 109, fasc. 132)." 2014. Available online at http://www.roger-pearse.com/weblog/2014/10/28/coptic-acts-of-andrew-and-paul-now-online-in-english/

———. "From Egyptian to Coptic: Religious Vocabulary." n.d. Available online at https://www.academia.edu/4583670/From_Egyptian_to_Coptic_Religious_Vocabulary

ARKELL, Anthony. "Varia Sudanica." *Journal of Egyptian Archaeology* 36 (1950): pp. 24–42.

———. *A History of the Sudan from the Earliest Times to 1821*. London, 1961.

ARMBRUSTER, C.H. *Dongolese Nubian: A Lexicon*. Cambridge: Cambridge University Press, 1965.

ATANASSOVA, Diliana. "Prinzipen und Kriterien für die Erforschung der koptischen liturgischen Typika des Schenuteklosters." In Σύναξις καθολική: *Beiträge zu Gottesdienst und Geschichte der fünf altkirchischen Patriarchate für Heinzgerd Brakmann zum 70. Geburtstag*, ed. D. Atanassova & T. Chronz. Berlin 2014: pp. 13–38.

BROWNE, Gerald M. "An Old Nubian Lectionary Fragment." *Orientalia* 70 (2001): pp. 113–16.

———. "An Old Nubian Version of the Liber Institutionis Michaelis." In *Coptic Studies: Acts of the 3rd International Congress of Coptic Studies, Warsaw, 20–25 August 1984*. Warsaw, 1990.

———. "A Revision of the Old Nubian Version of the *Institutio Michaelis*." *Beiträge zur Sudanforschung* 3 (1988): pp. 17–24.

———. *Bibliorum Sacrorum Versio Palaeonubiana* [= CSCO 547]. Louvain: Peeters, 1994.

———. *Chrysostomus Nubianus: An Old Nubian Version of Ps. Chryso-stom, In venerabilem crucem sermo* [= *Papyrologica Castroctaviana* 10]. Rome & Barcelona, 1984.

———. *Griffith's Old Nubian Lectionary* [= *Papyrologica Castroctavi-ana* 8]. Roma & Barcelona, 1982.

———. *Literary Texts in Old Nubian* [= *Beiträge zur Sudanforschung - Beiheft* 5]. Vienna, 1989.

———. "Miscellanea Nubiana (II)." *Orientalia* 64 (1995): pp. 450–59.

———. *Old Nubian Dictionary*. Louvain: Peeters, 1996.

———. *Old Nubian Grammar* [= *Languages of the World/Materials* 330]. Munich: Lincom Europa, 2002.

———. "Old Nubian Literature." In *Études nubiennes: Conférence de Genève, Actes du VIIᵉ Congrès international d'études nubiennes, 3–8 septembre 1990, I: Communications principales*, edited by Ch. Bon-net. Geneva, 1992.

———. *Old Nubian Texts from Qasr Ibrim 2*. London, 1989.

———. *Old Nubian Texts from Qasr Ibrim 3*. London, 1991.

———. "The Sunnarti Luke." *Zeitschrift für Papyrologie und Epigraphik* 77 (1989): pp. 293–96.

CHITTICK, H.N. "Antiquities of the Batn el Hajjar." *Kush* v (1957): pp. 42–48.

CRUM, W.E. *A Coptic Dictionary*. Oxford, 1939.

VAN GERVEN OEI, Vincent W.J. "The Old Nubian Memorial for King George." In *Nubian Voices: Studies in Christian Nubian Culture*, edited by Adam Łajtar and Jacques van der Vliet [= *The Journal of Juristic Papyrology Supplement* XV]. Warsaw: Raphael Tauben-schlag Foundation, 2011: pp. 225–62.

———. "Remarks toward a Revised Grammar of Old Nubian." *Dotawo* 1 (2014): pp. 165–84.

———. "Old Nubian Relative Clauses." *Dotawo* 2 (2015): pp. 9–57.

———. "A Note on the Old Nubian Morpheme -ⲁ in Nominal and Verba Predicates" In *Nubian Voices II: New Texts and Stud-ies on Christian Nubian Culture*, edited by Adam Łajtar, Grze-gorz Ochała, and Jacques van der Vliet [= *The Journal of Juristic Papyrology Supplement* XXVII]. Warsaw: Raphael Taubenschlag Foundation, 2015: pp. 313–34.

———. *A Possible Grammar of Old Nubian*. Louvain: Peeters, in preparation.

———. "Old Nubian Prosody and Assimilation." In preparation.

——— & El-Shafie EL-GUZUULI. *The Miracle of Saint Mina*. The Hague: Uitgeverij, 2013.

GRIFFITH, Francis Ll. "The Nubian Texts of the Christian Period." In *Proceedings of the British Academy* 14 (1928): 117–46.

HAGEN, Joost. "The Diaries of the Apostles: 'Manuscript Find' and 'Manuscript Fiction' in Coptic Homilies and Other Literary Texts." In *Coptic Studies on the Threshold of the New Millennium: Proceedings of the Seventh International Congress of Coptic Studies, Leiden, 27 August - 2 September 2002*, 2 vols., edited by Mat Immerzeel and Jacques van der Vliet [= OLA 133]. Louvain: Peeters, 2004: pp. 349–67.

————. "Districts, Towns and Other Locations of Medieval Nubia and Egypt, Mentioned in the Coptic and Old Nubian Texts from Qasr Ibrim." *Sudan & Nubia* 13 (2009): pp. 114–19.

———— and Grzegorz OCHAŁA. "Saints and Scriptures for Phaophi: Preliminary Edition of and Commentary on a Typikon Fragment from Qasr Ibrim." In Σύναξις καθολική: *Beiträge zu Gottesdienst und Geschichte der fünf altkirchischen Patriarchate für Heinzgerd Brakmann zum 70. Geburtstag*, ed. D. Atanassova & T. Chronz. Berlin, 2014: pp. 269–90.

JAKOBI, Angelika, and El-Shafie EL-GUZUULI. "Semantic Change and Heterosemy of Dongolawi *ed*." *Dotawo* 1 (2014): pp. 121–44.

JAKOBIELSKI, Stefan. "The inscriptions, Ostraca and Graffiti," In D.A. Welsby & C.M. Daniels, *Soba: Archaeological Research at a Medieval Capital on the Blue Nile*. London, 1991: pp. 274–96.

KHALIL, Mokhtar M. *Wörterbuch der nubischen Sprache (Fadidja/ Mahas-Dialekt)*. Warsaw, 1996.

ŁAJTAR, Adam. "Old Nubian Texts from Gebel Adda in the Royal Ontario Museum," *Dotawo* 1 (2014): pp. 185–201.

ŁAPTAŚ, Magdalena. "Archangels as Protectors and Guardians in Nubian Painting." In *Between the Cataracts: Proceedings of the 11th International Conference for Nubian Studies, Warsaw University, 27 August-2 September 2006, Part Two: Session Papers*, 2 vols., eds. W. Godlewski & A. Łajtar. Warsaw, 2010: pp. 675–81.

LEPSIUS, Karl R. *Nubische Grammatik*. Berlin, 1880.

VON MASSENBACH, Gertrude. "Wörterbuch des nubischen Kunuzi-Dialektes mit einer grammatischen Einleitung." *Mitteilungen des Seminars für Orientalische Sprachen zu Berlin* 36.3 (1933): 99–227.

MILLS, A.J. "The Reconnaissance Survey from Gemai to Dal: A Preliminary Report for 1963–64", *Kush* XIII (1965): pp. 6–7

MÜLLER, C.D.G. *Die Bücher der Einsetzung der Erzengel Michael und Gabriel* [= CSCO 225-226 (Copt. 31-32)]. Louvain: Peeters, 1962.

OCHAŁA, Grzegorz. "Multilingualism in Christian Nubia: Qualitative and Quantitative Approaches." *Dotawo* 1 (2014): pp. 1–50.

OLIVER, Harold H. "The Epistle of Eusebius to Carpianus: Textual Tradition and Translation." *Novum Testamentum* 3 (1959): pp. 138–45

PARKER, D.C. *An Introduction to the New Testament Manuscripts and Their Texts*. Cambridge: Cambridge University Press, 2008.

PLUMLEY, J.Martin, and Gerald M. BROWNE. *Old Nubian Texts from Qasr Ibrīm I*. London, 1988.

QUECKE, H. "Zwei Blätter aus koptischen Hermeneia-Typika in der Papyrussamlung der Österrichischen Nationalbibliothek (P. Vindob. K 9725 und 9734)." *Papyrus Erzherzog Rainer: Festschrift zum 100-jährigen Bestehen der Papyrussamlung der Österrichischen Nationalbibliothek*. Vienna, 1983, Textband, pp. 194–206 & Tafelband, taf. 14–16.

REINISCH, Leo. *Die Nuba-Sprache. Erster Theil: Grammatik und Texte*. Vienna, 1879.

———. *Die Nuba-Sprache. Zweiter Theil: Nubisch-Deutsches und Deutsch-Nubisches Wörterbuch*. Vienna, 1879.

RILLY, Claude. *Le méroïtique et sa famille linguistique* [= Collection Afrique et Language 14]. Louvain: Peeters, 2010.

RUFFINI, Giovanni. *Medieval Nubia: A Social and Economic History*. Oxford: Oxford University Press, 2012.

———. *The Bishop, the Eparch, and the King: Old Nubian Texts from Qasr Ibrim (P. QI IV)* [= The Journal of Juristic Papyrology Supplement XXII]. Warsaw: Raphael Taubenschlag Foundation, 2014.

SUCIU, Alin. *Apocryphon Berolinense/Argentoratense (Previously Known as the Gospel of the Savior). Reedition of P. Berol. 22220, Strasbourg Copte 5-7 and Qasr el-Wizz Codex ff. 12v-17r with Introduction and Commentary*. Unpublished dissertation. Université de Laval, Québec, 2013.

TROPPER, Joseph. *Altäthiopisch. Eine Grammatik des Ge'ez mit Übungstexten und Glossar*. [= Elementa Linguarum Orientis 2]. Münster, Ugarit-Verlag 2002.

TSAKOS, Alexandros. "The Cult of the Archangel Michael in Nubia." In preparation.

———. "The Liber Institutionis Michaelis in Medieval Nubia." *Dotawo* 1 (2014): pp. 51–62.

———. *The Greek Manuscripts on Parchment discovered at site SR022.A in the Fourth Cataract region, North Sudan*. Unpublished doctoral thesis. Humboldt University, Berlin, 2013.

———. *The Manuscripts discovered at SR022.A, North Sudan*. London: Golden House Publications, in preparation.

———. "The Textual Record from Serra East." In *Excavations at Serra East, George R. Hughes and James E. Knudstad, Directors. Part 9: Cerre Matto, the Christian Period and Later Pottery, Glass, Small Objects, Texts, and Inscribed Objects*, edited by Bruce Williams [= The University of Chicago Oriental Institute Nubian Expedition XIII]. Chicago: The Oriental Institute, forthcoming.

VAN DER VLIET, Jacques. "'What Is Man?': The Nubian Tradition of Coptic Funerary Inscriptions." In *Nubian Voices: Studies in Christian Nubian Culture*, edited by Adam Łajtar and Jacques van der Vliet [= *The Journal of Juristic Papyrology Supplement* xv]. Warsaw: Raphael Taubenschlag Foundation, 2011: pp. 171–224.

WERNER, Roland. *Grammatik des Nobiin (Nilnubisch): Phonologie, Tonologie und Morphologie.* Hamburg: Helmut Buske, 1987.

WEBER, Kerstin, and Petra WESCHENFELDER. "'Orakelpriester' oder 'patrolmen'? Eine altnubische Entlehnung im Text der Nastasen-Stele." *Lingua Aegyptia* 13. Göttingen (2005): pp. 173–79.

———. "Reflections on Old Nubian Grammar." *Dotawo* 1 (2014): pp. 83–92.

WEBER-THUM, Kerstin and Petra WESCHENFELDER. "The Multi-functional -ⲁ: A Wild-Card in Old Nubian Grammar?" In *Nubian Voices II: New Texts and Studies on Christian Nubian Culture*, edited by Adam Łajtar, Grzegorz Ochała, and Jacques van der Vliet [= *The Journal of Juristic Papyrology Supplement* xxvii]. Warsaw: Raphael Taubenschlag Foundation, 2015: pp. 301–12.

WESCHENFELDER, Petra. "Ceramics." In S. Haddow & M. Nicholas "The 2014 Season of Excavations at Kurgus," *Sudan & Nubia* 18 (2014): pp. 152–53.

———. "Ceramics." In A. Ginns, "The 2015 Season of Excavations at Kurgus," *Sudan & Nubia* 19 (2015): pp. 139–42.

ZOEGA, G. *Catalogus codicum copticorum manu scriptorum qui in Museo Borgeano Velitris adversantur.* Rome, 1810.

Made in the USA
Monee, IL
11 March 2022

92729374R00059